ADD VALUE
OR
STAY HOME

Turn your business "Outside-In"

Howard E. Hyden

FOREWORD

There are three classes of people:
those who see,
those who see when they are shown,
those who do not see.
- Leonardo da Vinci

"Outside-in" is a way of thinking. It's not customer service. It's looking at every facet of your business and asking: How does this add value for the customer, from the customer's point of view?

This book will change, forever, how you look at your business."

Every once in a while you meet someone like Howard, who "gets it." Howard knows with conviction what must be done if we wish to control the quality and velocity of our business. Sure, Howard taught us many practical solutions, but when you start thinking "outside-in," you have the key to making things go right in your business. Let me share with you some of the things this way of thinking has brought to our business.

At Westrec Marinas we are not in the boat storage business. We are in the Hospitality business. We are playing host to the recreational boating experience.

We deliver and compete on value, not price, and we are always finding ways to add value.

We tailor our products, practices, and services to meet our customers' needs. We know what our customers really want because of the way we ask them.

Well-trained, happy employees deliver the best service experience. Employees are our most valuable asset and we treat them that way.

All of our employees look at their job through the eyes of the customer.

At Westrec Marinas, we are customer focused and we do everything from the "outside-in."

These things are all merely the tip of the iceberg with regard to what Howard's information has brought to our business. This book is filled with anecdotes, case studies, principles, tips, warnings and more from Howard's enormous experience; experience that has helped to keep Westrec ahead of its time and ahead of the competition.

I hope you take advantage of the information in this book – providing, of course, that you're not our competition in the Marina business! This book will change, forever, how you look at your business.

If you ever get the opportunity to pick Howard's brain in person, count yourself very fortunate and take advantage of that opportunity.

All the best to you and all the best with your business endeavors,

Bill Anderson,
President
Westrec Marinas Management, Inc.

DEDICATION

To my amazing wife and children,

who all strive to play the game of life

at an awesome level.

INTRODUCTION

We make a living by what we get,
we make a life by what we give.
- Winston Churchill

My father, Hans Hyden, shaped my life. I can still hear him saying, "Son, worry about what you contribute to an organization rather than what you can take from it." Dad was referring to Boy Scouts, church groups and any other organization we were part of. He was the ultimate giver.

Dad encouraged us to do a good job at whatever we tackled. If I heard it once, I heard it a thousand times: "If a job is worth doing, it's worth doing right." He was a milkman and during the summer months, while I was going to college, I covered the routes for the milkmen who were on vacation. Since Dad encouraged me to give the best possible service, I had to figure out what I could do for the customer. When I loaded my truck in the morning, I made sure I had extra ice and I cut up pieces of cardboard so I could prop up the ice over the milk jugs for those customers that weren't early risers. That way they were sure to have cold milk and it wouldn't spoil in the summer heat.

My mother, Edythe, also instilled the values of being a giver. Her dedication to her children was enormous and there was never anything too small or too big that she wouldn't do for us. And she did the same for others. I also owe a debt of gratitude to Mom for whatever humor makes its way into my presentations. Mom was very funny and always made us laugh.

I am also grateful to other members of my family, who instilled in me values that have greatly contributed to my success. I owe a huge thank you to my aunt,

Anita Hallquist, who articulated my gift and abilities even though I had no clue. Early in my career, I was an instructor of large-scale computer systems. Aunt Anita was a manager of an apartment complex. I lived in the apartment with her and my uncle Thorvald. Frequently, I would have computer circuitry diagrams laid out all over her living room floor, studying what I was going to teach the next day. When tenants stopped in to pay their rent, she would introduce them to me. "This is my nephew Howard. He is an instructor of large-scale computer systems." The tenants were usually in awe and would say things like, "That must be really difficult" or "You must be really smart." This was back in the 60s when the public knew very little about computers compared to today. They thought you needed to be Einstein to work on computers. I usually responded by saying, "Computers are really not that difficult to understand. First of all, they really do not think for themselves." This was a common misconception at the time; computers only do what people, programmers, instruct them to do. Then I would proceed to explain how computers worked. The tenants would leave with a basic understanding. Aunt Anita would then say to me, "Young man, you have a tremendous gift and you don't have a clue as to what it is. You speak graphically. You have the ability of taking a very complex subject, such as computers, and with your graphic choice of words, you paint a picture in the listener's mind. You do not speak like a Harvard professor who is trying to impress everyone with a sophisticated vocabulary. You speak so that the typical person listening to you 'gets it.' That is a rare skill." Aunt Anita was right; I didn't have a clue. Evidently, when the clue train came by, I didn't get on it!

My Aunt Eunice also helped in honing my skills. When I was in college, she would take the letters I wrote, correct them with her red pen and mail them back to me. I was studying electrical engineering and writing was not my strong suit. I am sure my mother and Aunt Eunice are sitting in heaven now, amazed that I'm writing a book, and my aunt probably has her red pen ready to correct my mistakes. All in all I can proudly say that, as I was growing up, I saw that all of my relatives strived to do the best job they possibly could whether they were a carpenter, a painter, a mother, or a milkman.

When I arrived in the business world, I carried this philosophy with me. I strove to contribute to others, including customers, fellow employees and anyone else I came in contact with. Our customers have given our staff—Kate, Pat, Denise, Brian and Carolyn—the nickname "Team Awesome," and they deserve it. Denise passed away recently; we all miss her and she will always be remembered for her amazing contribution to our team.

In business, I believe the customer should be the teacher, and I have been fortunate enough to be the student of many great customers. They have taught me much of what I know. To paraphrase a popular leadership principle: "If you want to be the king, don't act like the king; act like the servant. If you act like the servant, you will become the king."

In this book we will explore how "outside-in" thinking will transform every facet of your business. We will look at how customer focus and customer service are light years apart. We will discuss the internal customer and the customer's customer. We will celebrate when things go well and knuckle down when things go horribly wrong. We will cheer for the heroes and pity the antagonists. Consider what the philosophy in this book could do for your business and keep reading.

Contents:

"Outside-In"
vs.
"Inside-Out"

*The real voyage of discovery consists not in seeking
new lands but in seeing with new eyes.*
- Marcel Proust

The Blank Tablet

*You cannot cut your
way to prosperity
- Howard*

When I was a corporate executive, the other executives were always having meetings about their financials – to put on the pressure with regard to increasing revenues, decreasing costs and increasing the bottom line.

While other executives were having yet another meeting on the P&L, I was out with my blank tablet (which I was often teased about), asking the customer to help define the play. I didn't want to play the game at the average level; I wanted to play the game at the awesome level, from the customer's perspective. This philosophy has grown to become my trademark, which is: "Dare to be Awesome . . . because the rest of the world is Average."

I would take my blank tablet and go out and talk to the customers and ask them what they wanted, when they needed it, what the hours of operation should be, what the lead time should

*Dare to be awesome...
because the rest of the
world is average - Howard*

1

be, etc. I wrote this information down, brought it back to the employees, and said, "That's the play." The customer has designed the play. The customer knows what they want. The customer knows what awesome is.

The term that I coined to describe this phenomenon was simply "outside-in." The problem, which is also an opportunity, is that the majority of companies look at their business through their own eyes, and the term I coined decades ago for this was "inside-out."

The majority of companies are "inside-out." Think about all the companies that you interact with when you are the customer. Are they "inside-out" or "outside-in"? Most companies expect the customer to walk to the beat of the company drum. I refer to this as "getting drunk on your own beer." Is your business drunk on its own beer?

It's interesting to me that the harder and more passionately we work for the customer, the luckier we get on the bottom line. You see, the key is to put the success of the customer first. If you do that, you will be astonished at how your sales and bottom line will grow.

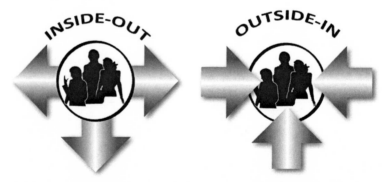

IS YOUR CUSTOMER MAKING YOU A COMMODITY?

One of the biggest problems facing companies competing in today's market environment is product parity. Some may refer to this as being a commodity or the commoditization of America. Some may refer to it as a "me-too." When the customer perceives your product or service to be the same as he or she can get from a competitor, you are in trouble. The only thing left is to compete on price. Most organizations really don't want to compete on price but they are forced to do so. If you don't want to compete on price, the only alternative is that you must "add value." **If you don't bring any more value to the party, *stay home*.**

Having a high quality product alone is probably not a competitive advantage. - Howard

Companies that implemented quality a decade ago had a decided competitive advantage. They had a quality product, zero defects, and got it to the customer on time. That used to be good enough to win in the market place, but the intensity of competition has become fierce. Even companies that were slow to adapt to the quality concept finally got their wakeup call when customers demanded it.

However, now the customer has developed the attitude that, "Everyone has the same stuff." This is what we call "product parity." Having a high quality product is no longer good enough to thrive in a competitive environment. It's only your ticket into the game, it doesn't allow you to win the game.

WHAT IS YOUR UNIQUE COMPETITIVE ADVANTAGE?

Most organizations realize that it is important to have a unique competitive advantage. It is rare that the product itself can be a unique competitive advantage, unless you are Apple and can come up with a constant stream of truly innovative gotta-have, way-cool products from the Mac to the iPod, iPhone, and now the iPad. Apple products are very cool fashion statements, incredibly user friendly, and the envy of all those that do not have them. Some companies may be fortunate enough to have patents or something that will protect them from having a competitor clone their product. However, most companies are not that fortunate. If they come out with a new product, it's amazing how fast the competition will come out with a similar product.

I also state that customer service is no longer a competitive advantage. When I speak at conferences and I make that statement, there is typically a stunned silence in the room. After all, speakers always talk about customer service.

Customer service is probably not a competitive advantage. - Howard

When I recently asked the president of an advertising agency what was her unique competitive advantage, she replied, "We have great relationships with our customers and we have excellent customer service."

I said, "Very good." Then I asked her how her competitors would answer that same question. The startled look on her face told me she realized where I was going with the conversation.

Most agency presidents, if they were being honest, would say, "My competitors are saying, 'We have great relationships with our customers and we have excellent customer service.'" Can you imagine a competitor saying, "We have horrible relationships with our customers and we suck on customer service?" So, in fact, the only way customer service can be a competitive advantage is if your competitors are pathetic at customer service.

The second problem with customer service is that it is very tactical and it's aimed at the customer contact person – usually the sales rep or the customer service rep. They concentrate on things like smiling at the customer when the customer walks in and calling the customer by name. And this is why I don't stress customer service.

I emphasize CUSTOMER FOCUS. It is light years apart from customer service and it's not tactical. It's strategic.

I am always looking for ways to increase an organization's competitive advantage. To do that, you can't just think sales and customer service; you have to think *strategically* and you have to think *organization-wide.*

IS YOUR FOCUS ON YOUR P&L?

I love to compete against those competitors who are obsessed with the bottom line. My experience is that many times the employees know what is the right thing to do, but management pushes the bottom line.

Remember…resist the temptation to follow the crowd by cutting expenses in all areas. I refer to this as counterintuitive thinking.

When the rest of the market cuts expenses, perhaps you should increase investments in strategic areas such as advertising, commissions, training, and value to the customer. Then smile all the way to the bank.

The problem is that too many companies have become obsessed with their P&L (Profit & Loss Statement.) If you continuously focus on your financials, you have the wrong stimulus. The administrative cost of practices based on "inside-out" thinking does not show up on your P&L—it's on the customer's P&L. You simply will not see the cost to the customer highlighted. If you focus on making your customers' financials look good, then your financials will begin to look good.

Tip: Replace a meeting about your P&L with a meeting to discuss your customer's P&L. Once a quarter, discuss what you can do to help your customer increase their revenue or reduce their operating cost. What might change in terms of customer requirements? Remember, if you have one meeting on your customer's P&L, you are still discussing your P&L twice as much as theirs. That doesn't seem too out of line— that is, if you want to be awesome.

DO YOU HAVE A PRODUCT LOOKING FOR A MARKET?

When the rest of the world goes south . . . perhaps you should go north. - Howard

Many businesses start in one of two ways: In the first scenario, you have some very intelligent and well-educated people graduating from top universities. They then use their knowledge to design a product. This group of people gets together and decides to build what the customer "ought to want." The thinking is, "We are the engineers. We went to Purdue. We went to MIT. We are the experts on this technology. We'll design it our way. By the way, what does the customer know anyway? So let's not ask them."

They sit down and make all the decisions on behalf of the customer and then they believe that the customer ought to want the product. They hire sales people to sell it and accounting people to keep score. Most organizations fall under this category. They have fallen in love with their product and feel that everyone should beat a path to their door to buy it. Inside the company, the employees make all the decisions on behalf of the customer and then they push their product out into the marketplace.

The other type of business mold is the entrepreneur who starts a company in their garage and builds a product to fill a need. These organizations have originated from the right mindset.

But most companies that I have seen fit the following phrase: "We have a product running around looking for a market." High tech companies are notorious for this. They have continuously built "what the customer ought to want." In many cases, they have over-engineered the product, making it "feature rich." Adding features that the product designers want, however, adds no real value if the customer doesn't see it that way. Along with the added cost comes the price increase.

However, when it comes right down to it, the company cannot increase the price because the customer is unwilling to pay for the extra "bells and whistles" that bring no value to him. The "feature-rich" product has now created profit margin erosion. I frequently tell clients "less is more." You no doubt can think of numerous examples of where the product has been over-engineered.

THE CUSTOMER IS RAISING THE BAR . . . ARE YOU?

When I was a corporate executive, prior to every budget cycle I required my management teams to conduct meetings to discuss what they were going to do to bring "more value" to the customer.

Every year management teams typically budget for the following year. They forecast an increase in revenue, higher margins, increased profits, etc. However, do they also make decisions on how they are going to bring "more value" to the customer? Rarely.

That value might be increased through higher on-time delivery percentage, shorter lead times, quicker turnaround times, etc. I expected them to schedule a meeting with me to present what this value looked like. What are the odds that they are going to bring more value to the customer if they haven't even spent twenty minutes talking about what that value would look like? Does "slim to none" come to mind?

The obvious question was, "Have you discussed this with any customers? Was it the customers who came up with these suggestions?" This customer meeting was crucial.

Are your customers going to raise the bar and demand more value next year?
- Howard

I typically ask conference audiences, "How many of you would say the customer is going to raise the bar and demand more value from your organization next year?" Every hand goes up. Next I ask, "How many of your companies have had a meeting to discuss what you are going to do to bring 'more value' to the customer next year?" Rarely do I get any raised hands on that one.

Tip: *Schedule a meeting now to discuss what your team is going to do to bring more value to your customers. Invite some customers. I am a major believer in having managers/executives do pre-work prior to the meeting so they are well prepared to discuss the topic. This would include having discussions with customers before the meeting.*

The only good news relative to not having a meeting to discuss bringing more value to the party is that your competitors have probably not had this meeting either. One of my clients referred to this observation as, "We are no worse than the competition." What kind of an answer is that?! **How average! Not awesome!**

Scheduling a meeting once a year prior to developing your budget might just be a bare minimum requirement. Since there are three months to a quarter, why not have two meetings on your financials and a third to discuss raising the bar on bringing more value to the customer?

DO YOU MAKE IT EASY FOR THE CUSTOMER?

Making things simple and customer-oriented is a way to add value for your customer. Don't over-design things. Most customers will just get frustrated. It seems like common sense; however, my observation is that there is nothing "common" about common sense.

Simplicity is the ultimate sophistication.
- Leonardo da Vinci

What percentage of adults in the United States does not know how to program their DVD player, TIVO, or whatever box they have connected to their TV? The actual answer is 90%. Yes, 90% of U.S. adults do not know how to program these devices. They're easy to spot: you walk in their house and the device is sitting on top of the TV going 12-blink-blink-blink. If they want it programmed, they give it to their kids and say, "You figure it out. I have no idea how to make this thing work."

Picture for a moment the remote control of a DVD player. It looks like the cockpit of a DC-10. Have you ever seen more buttons in your life? Can't you just imagine the engineers sitting back and having a conversation like this…? "Let's add a button to do this; let's add another button to do that; and oh, how about a button to do this other thing…that would be brilliant. This chip has an incredible amount of power. Let's program it to do everything under the sun."

Does anyone really believe that adding another button or programming that chip to do something else actually adds value for the customer? The majority of us would not think it adds any value at all. In fact, here's an interesting question. How many believe that it actually detracts from the value for the customer? So, now they have detracted from the value and, by the way, what have they done to the cost? Obviously they've increased the cost. It's called "over-engineering" or "feature rich."

OUR MULTIMEDIA GUIDE

At our house, we have a typical home entertainment system that includes the TV, DVD, stereo amplifier and cable box. We have four remote controls to operate the system. It was often very confusing to figure out which remote control to pick up, let alone what buttons to push.

The key is: "more is not better" —"better is better" and better is always defined by the customer. - Howard

So, being in the value-added business, I saw an opportunity here to add some serious value. I scanned all the remote controls into my computer, resulting in digital images. I then designed a booklet with instructions on how to execute the various functions. I took the first remote and drew an arrow to Step 1: push this button. On the next remote, Step 2: push this button. On the next one: Step 3: push this button; and so on. Then on the next page, I put the buttons they would need to push in order to watch regular TV. There was another section for the cable box and surround sound, etc.

When people came to our house, they were curious about the title of this little booklet, "The Multimedia Guide for Non-Techies." As soon as they understood what it was, their comments were inevitably the same: "Would you design one for my house?"

The question is, "Does this booklet add value for the customer?" Far too many companies are only interested in the product they have designed. They spend a significant amount of time focusing on their product or service and very little time focusing on what would add value for the customer.

The above example is a classic illustration where companies have focused on their technical product but not focused on "adding-value." The "Multimedia Guide for Non-Techies" clearly adds significant value and yet the cost is minimal.

IVY ACRES

Ivy Acres has grown into one of the major suppliers of bedding plants in the northeast. They sell to retailers such as Home Depot.

One way in which Ivy Acres makes it easier for the consumer involves the use of a new type of pot. Ivy Acres announced the introduction of their new, patent pending, biodegradable "Straw" plant pot. The new potting system is made from rice straw, coconut fiber and natural latex adhesive. What makes this product so exciting is that all of its materials are natural—waste by-products of rice and coconut production. These raw materials are in plentiful supply. They are normally indiscriminately disposed of, since there has been no significant use for them.

StrawPots are available in several standard sizes and shapes. Growers can confidently plant directly in the StrawPots and ship them off to their retail customers without concern for the integrity of the pot. Once the consumer plants them, the  pots begin to degrade in less than a year. They naturally biodegrade and form soil-enriching compost. From an ecological standpoint, the major advantage of StrawPots is that growers no longer need to pot in plastic containers that need to be removed and discarded after planting. This new system is not only more customer friendly, it is also more environmentally friendly.

THE TWO STEPS TO CUSTOMER FOCUS

I define customer focus in two steps:

Step One:
Every single employee in the company must look at their job through the eyes of the customer. Whether they have contact with the customer in person, over the phone, or not at all, is irrelevant. So, whether they are the truck driver, the bookkeeper, the nurse or doctor, the I.T. person, or the engineer, they must look at their job through the eyes of the customer. In other words, all employees must be "outside-in."

Step Two:

Every employee must "add value" on top of the product. The wrong comparison would be: "I'm the electrician; how do I add value compared to sales or customer service?" I would refer to that as apples to oranges. They are comparing themselves against a different function in their own company. The proper comparison would be: "I am the electrician; how do I add more value on top of the product compared to the electrician at the competitor's company?"

ARE YOU INSIDE-OUT OR OUTSIDE-IN?

What questions do you get over and over again from your customers?

You probably get the same question 250 times a year, albeit from different customers. The point is, you have to answer the same questions over and over again. Identify what those questions are, document them, and then figure out a way to provide quick and easily accessible answers to your customers.

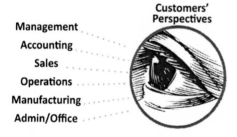

Customers'
Perspectives

Management
Accounting
Sales
Operations
Manufacturing
Admin/Office

Example: A mortgage company determined that the first-time home buyer had many questions and frequently made several trips before they finally got their loan application put together properly. The employees decided that they could create a DVD for the first-time homebuyer. On that DVD would be everything a first-timer would need to know in order to properly put together their loan application—such things as termite inspections, credit reports, etc. This made it much easier for their prospects to complete loan applications and it instantly became a differentiator from other mortgage companies. Now their new customers became PWOM (Positive Word Of Mouth) sales reps. Every time their friends or acquaintances talked about buying a home, they would share the example of how easy it was because of the DVD.

Management
Accounting
Sales
Operations
Manufacturing
Admin/Office

Quality Products

In the box below, write the question(s) your organization gets hundreds of times per year. Then brainstorm with your teammates on how to disseminate the information the customer needs.

Question:

Now, let's contrast "inside-out" or a product-driven culture with the opposite: "outside-in" or a customer-focused culture. As human beings, it is quite natural for us to look at everything through our own eyes. This means we default to an "inside-out" perspective. It is extremely difficult to discover areas that would "add value" for the customer when we design everything looking through our own eyes.

When we shift the organizational culture to an "outside-in" perspective, our ability to discover "added-value" goes up exponentially. If you are customer focused, you go out in the marketplace. (It is the only place I know where there are customers. They're not hanging around the office.) Find out how the customers want it, when they want it, etc. Let the customers determine the specs. Bring that information back to the company and do it the customers' way. I call this "outside-in." It means you look at the business by standing in the customers' shoes and looking at your business through the customers' eyes.

AN INCREDIBLE EXAMPLE OF CUSTOMER FOCUS

"Outside-in" means a thorough understanding of the customers' needs and making everything "easy for the customer." Customers do not want hassles. In the 60s, I was an engineer on, what were then, supercomputers. I'm not the smartest computer geek in the world. That distinction may go to a person like Seymour Cray, who was one of the founders of the company I worked for. During my stint in the Navy, I was responsible for all of the electronic communications utilized to recover two astronauts. I am able to handle technology. I could probably handle any computer available in today's market place. However, I choose to use Apple computers. Why? Because they are far more user-friendly. We have Macs throughout my company and at home. I've convinced relatives, as well as business people, to switch to Mac because they are customer focused.

11

Example: When I speak or do a workshop, it wouldn't be that difficult for me to trip over the power cord of my laptop. Apple has anticipated this problem for the customer, and designed a solution: the MagSafe Power Adapter. When the power cord gets tripped over, it will easily detach from the computer, so that the computer does not go careening across the room or stage.

Another Example: Early on, Apple's strategy, in terms of third-party developers, was to have them use the exact same menu bars at the top, regardless of what software was being used. Once the user is familiar with that look, they can use that knowledge in the next application, making it easier for non-geeks to use their Mac.

Just think about the now infamous series of Apple commercials featuring PC and Mac. The two of them are sitting in their own box. The Apple guy jumps out and says, "I'm plugged in and I'm ready to go!" This speaks to the audience and says, "Mac is easy!" Every time they have trouble with their PC, the TV spot is in the back of their mind whispering, "It's easy to use Apple technology." Apple has successfully built an environment of "Mac is cool; Mac is easy."

Apple's designs are incredible. Look at the iMac. Look at the iPhone and iPad. They are classic examples of "cool looking design" married with technologies that are very easy to use. When Steve Jobs introduced the iPhone, his presentation illustrated how simple it was for the customer to use the product. He took his finger and scrolled up and down music titles. He demonstrated how easy, fun and cool it is to use the iPhone.

Frequently, after delivering a presentation at a conference or Association meeting, attendees will approach me afterwards and state, "Wow, your slides were really awesome. How did you get PowerPoint to do that?" I have a standard response, which is, "I don't use PowerPoint. I am an over-the-top Apple guy. I use their program called Keynote." I then say, "Keynote is PowerPoint on steroids. I much prefer using Keynote because it is much more user-friendly, and it allows me to do some awesome things with my presentations." I then sometimes say, "If you gave me a PC, I would donate it to the Salvation Army." I have probably said that at least a thousand times in front of tens of thousands of people. Why would I downgrade to a PC when I can do awesome stuff with my Macs?

There are a whole bunch of reasons why I am a PWOM (Positive Word Of Mouth) advocate for Apple. My staff has frequently reminded me that there's probably only one person who is more passionate about the Mac than I am, and his name is Steve Jobs.

Techies should not design products for techies. They should design products for non-techies and make it easy for the customer to use their products. All companies should take a lesson from Apple and design their products so they're customer friendly. This would eliminate frustration on the part of the end-user. Techies and engineers have a tendency to over-engineer products. Just yesterday, in writing this book, I said, "How do I get rid of this stupid TV with a paperclip?" I said, "This guy pops up one more time to give me a hand and…I'm going to shoot him!" Have you ever thought the same thing?

So, is your organization "inside-out" or "outside-in"? Wait, don't answer that. What would your customers say? That's the proof in the pudding.

Customer Service is Tactical, Customer Focus is Strategic

Human subtlety will never devise an invention
more beautiful, more simple or more direct
than does nature, because in her inventions
nothing is lacking, and nothing is superfluous.
- Leonardo da Vinci

Customer Focus, Not Customer Service

Customer service is typically described as the relationship between the contact person and the customer. As an example, when I check into the Marriott Hotel and put my credit card on the counter, the employee looks at me, gives me a nice smile, and says, "Welcome to the Marriott, Mr. Hyden." Although this is nice, it is not a unique competitive advantage. Why? Because when I check into the Holiday Inn, the Hilton or the Doubletree they all do the same thing. Greeting the customer by their name with a friendly smile is not a great differentiator, unless your competitors are pathetic. Personally, I've never been one that wants to win because the competitor is pathetic.

In most companies, customer service training is targeted at those employees that have direct contact with the customer, either in person or on the phone. It rarely encompasses the other functions in the company. In fact, if you have a department called "customer service," this can be a trap. Why? Because the people in the other departments might well think, "Customer service handles the customers; I'm not involved with that area." This is "inside-out" thinking.

15

Customer focus, on the other hand, represents an entire shift in the culture of the organization to one that is "outside-in." Policies, procedures, how we do business here – everything is driven by looking at the business through the eyes of the customer.

HAVE YOU OVER-DESIGNED?

Inside-out: For two decades, Sandhill Scientific, a Colorado-based medical device manufacturer, had lived in the world of inside-out thinking, particularly with regard to how products were engineered and brought to market. Several of the company's products—a line of diagnostic systems used mainly by gastroenterologists—were computer-based. In the mid-90s many companies were going through the changeover to allow computer screens to present a graphical user interface with icons and pull-down menus. Complemented by the ability to enter computer commands via the use of a mouse, it truly was a revolution.

Sandhill was no exception. Wanting to take advantage of this new format, they launched a fairly aggressive project to transition to a new system. Halfway through the project, the company was educated on the fallacy of inside-out thinking. Though considerable work had been done in moving toward the new system, it was obvious the new product, to be called "InSIGHT," was more of a "computer" than a "medical device." While InSIGHT would or could have all sorts of "bells and whistles," it required nurses to become computer operators as opposed to healthcare providers. In effect, the product had been designed by engineers, for engineers—engineers that "went wild" with all of the capabilities offered by the new platform. Realizing this, the company scrapped the transition project and started over. They pulled out the proverbial "blank sheet of paper" . . . but they didn't write anything on it; they left it blank. The authors and designers of what would go on this paper would be Sandhill's customers themselves.

Nurses from the Front Range area of Colorado were brought to a series of one-day meetings at Sandhill. The first part of the day was a "downloading" session (this is a kind word; the real word rhymes with "witching"—these were "witching sessions"). Discussions centered on such topics as: "What did the nurses like about doing the procedure associated with a product like InSIGHT? What was cumbersome? What was confusing? What took too much time? What was frustrating?"

The second half of the day focused on solutions, and this is where items began to appear on the paper. What would make the procedure easier and less confusing? What would make it quicker? The design of the new InSIGHT began to take shape. This was all-inclusive . . . i.e., not just what the software would do, but how each component of the system would be arranged and presented for the user (for example, the type of stand or cart that would be used, where the monitor would be located, and so forth.)

This design team of nurses was highly successful. The user interface did not contain pull-down menus or require a mouse. Instead, the display showed the nurse only those items she needed at each phase of the diagnostic procedure. It actually walked the nurse through the procedure in what became known as a "guided protocol." The computer was controlled via the use of a touch screen with relatively large "buttons" on the display. Again, only the buttons required for each particular portion of the procedure were shown at a given time. In effect, the procedure was greatly simplified and the time required was shortened. When Sandhill's sales force demonstrated the system, they let the nurse do the "demo." The guided protocol was so simple and straightforward that even a nurse unfamiliar with the procedure could easily accomplish it! The "top line" result: once the new InSIGHT hit the marketplace Sandhill's revenues jumped 42%!

Computer operating systems can be simple and customer-friendly. How's that for an oxymoron?

As I've already mentioned, I am a major fan of Apple and its products. I was an engineer on large-scale computers, and in my prior life some even referred to me as a "propeller head." Despite the fact that I have the technical skills to figure out how to use any operating system, why would I want the frustration? Apple's new operating system, OSX Leopard, is a classic example of "customer-focused engineering." Leopard is architected from the user in, rather than from the technology out. Too many products today—computers as well as many other products—are designed by product development people according to what the customer "ought to want," as opposed to designing it from the customer's perspective. However, it should be all about making it easier for the customer, and Apple is the poster child for this approach in the technology arena. I am confident that when their new operating system, "Lion," comes out, it will roar customer friendly. Since they have now become the highest market cap company, this strategy is obviously paying handsome dividends.

DO YOU PREDICT YOUR CUSTOMERS' NEEDS?

When Boeing designed its 777 aircraft, they took a different approach. They decided to involve the customer in helping them with the design. Having designed previous aircraft, such as the 747 or 757, it is easy to see why Boeing felt they were experts at designing aircraft.

A tremendous amount of knowledge and experience can be the organization's competitive advantage. However, this knowledge and experience can too frequently lead to tunnel vision and, therefore, easily become a competitive disadvantage. This is called "getting blind-sided by your own expertise." The myopic view might be, "How could a flight attendant possibly teach us how to build an aircraft?" Regardless of how intelligent, educated or experienced we are, we need to become much better students and let the customer teach us how to design an awesome product.

We need to become the student and let our customers become the teacher. - Howard

Have you ever been a customer of an organization and thought, "I could design a more awesome play than these people?" No doubt the answer is a resounding "YES!" The question is, "Did they ask for your ideas on how to design a more awesome play?" I'll assume that was a "no" answer. You had the ability to teach them the play; however, they never asked you. It hasn't occurred to them to become the student and let you be the teacher . . . another missed opportunity. They know it all! Isn't it amazing how many companies "know it all"?

When designing the 777, Boeing interviewed several different groups of their customers' employees. During a session with flight attendants, some of the flight attendants indicated that when a reading light burned out, replacing the bulb was a needlessly complicated process. They filled out a maintenance request form with the seat number, as well as the serial number of the aircraft. This form was then processed through their chain of command and then the maintenance chain of command. Ultimately, a mechanic would service the aircraft by taking apart the light fixture, removing the old bulb and replacing it with a new one, and then fastening the light fixture back in its original position. Undoubtedly, additional paperwork would be submitted documenting this service procedure. The flight attendants said, "Why not design the light fixture so that when a bulb burns out in flight, we can get a spare from the galley and change it right then and there?" What a concept! There are incremental costs to having the flight attendants fill out a maintenance request form and having a mechanic change the light bulb. And then there is an incremental cost to the customer but there is no incremental added value. Not only is there incremental cost to the customer, but meanwhile the passenger has been reading in the dark. Therefore, the customers' customer loses as well.

Tip: *Have a meeting titled "What Can We Do to Reduce the Total Cost for the Customer?" Quantify this number, if possible. Could you include this number in your next proposal? Would this help increase your close rate? The focus on helping your customers' bottom line just might increase yours.*

Boeing met with another group of their customers' employees. These were the people that analyze the number of passengers traveling to the various cities: how many were in coach, how many in first class, how many were international passengers. When customers purchased airliners prior to the 777, they could specify the number of first-class seats and the number of coach seats. For example, the airline might want 10 first-class seats, so Boeing would build the plane with 10 first-class seats. However, in meeting with people who planned the airline's loading, they were told that loading may change and therefore they may need more first-class seats. Prior to the 777, the airline was stuck with the configuration they originally ordered. As a result of getting input from this group, the Boeing engineers designed the 777 so that the wall between first-class and coach was movable. Should the airline suddenly have more flights to international destinations requiring more first-class seats, they could simply remove some of the coach seats and then slide the wall between first-class and coach, including the restroom, toward the rear of the plane and install more first-class seats. The result would be an increase in revenue for the airlines. Does this add more value to American and Lufthansa?

KEY POINT:

Average: If you are average, you understand what your customers' requirements are today.

Awesome: If you want to play the game at the awesome level, you must understand how your customers' requirements might change. Then you would design your product or service to meet your customers' future needs. Focus more on helping your customers increase their revenue. Then your revenue may also go up. Too many companies are self-serving, focusing on their own success rather than that of their customers.

I received a phone call from my insurance rep informing me that my insurance was about to expire and that I needed to get a check in the mail immediately. I let him know that I hadn't even looked at the policy and that

I have learned a lot since I knew it all.
- Howard

I was out of town. He said that if I could just send the amount now he could adjust it later; that way he wouldn't have a chargeback on his commission. I wondered, "Is this guy for real!?" Having a pretty good network in place, I sent out an SOS for the best insurance guy in Colorado Springs; the response was Randy Kilgore. After contacting him and explaining the situation he sent me the quote for what I would have received from the other agency, and then he also informed me that because of my age I could save a substantial amount of money if I changed the policy term from 10 to 15 years. He wasn't trying to up-sell; he was just laying out the facts for me. He was looking at my future needs.

HOW DO YOU MEET YOUR CUSTOMER'S UNIQUE NEEDS?

One Size Does Not Fit All. When my son was young he had surgery in Minnesota, nothing life threatening. As we sat in the lobby of the hospital, the staff brought him out and I started cracking up. My wife, Dorothy, was elbowing me to knock it off, and I thought any minute there would be another surgical procedure needed to repair my broken rib. Why was I laughing? I was absolutely convinced that they put my second grader in the exact same gown that some Minnesota Viking linebacker would wear, or someone about 6'9" and 350 lbs. One size fits all?

When my daughter was born, my wife needed a cesarean section. Surgery is in the front; the opening in the gown is in the back. Is that stupid or what? That might give a new definition to ICU.

Now this company makes gowns for little folks, and they have another gown with cotton buttons in the front so the surgeon can easily get to the tummy. What do you suppose has happened to sales in this company? Different customers have different needs and they want products designed to accommodate their particular needs.

Tip: *Has your company fallen into the trap of "One size fits all"? Have a meeting to discuss the diverse needs of your customers, and then redesign your product to meet the unique needs of different customer segments.*

DEMOGRAPHICS ARE VITAL TO THE DESIGN PROCESS

Sometimes in order to find awesome value, you may need to look at your business not only through your customers' eyes, but also through the *demographics* of your customers.

CONSIDER AGE

Let's take a look at a business through the eyes of the senior citizen.

Another client of ours, Del Webb Corporation, built retirement communities in warm climates. One had to be at least 55 years old to live at Del Webb. An electrician's job is to install electrical outlets in every room in the house. Obviously, we need electricity for various appliances in every room. While doing a workshop for Del Webb, I looked at a young man who was an electrician and I asked him how old he was. He responded, "Twenty-seven years old."

I said, "Therein lies the problem. You are looking at your job through the eyes of a twenty-seven-year-old. How high do you install the electrical outlets?" His response was, "Ten to twelve inches from the floor." I asked him to pretend that his grandmother, who is seventy years old, came to him and whispered in his ear how high to put the outlets. What would she say?

After pausing for a moment he said, "Probably higher, maybe thirty inches off the floor." When you are over 55 you don't bend as well as you did before. Would putting the outlets higher add value to the customer? Of course it would. Does this cost Del Webb money, or save them money? It actually saves them money. The wire usually comes from the ceiling, not through the floor, so they use fewer materials. Secondly, consider an electrician who is installing outlets at thirty inches off the floor vs. another electrician who is installing at ten inches off the floor. Which one is going to get done faster?

Another example: Every one of us probably has a 2-position switch by the front door. It's pretty basic; it turns your porch light on and off. However, that's average. Let's play the game at the awesome level. At Del Webb, they have a 3-position switch: on, off and the middle position. If you have any type of medical emergency, and you have dialed 911 and the ambulance is on the way, put the switch in the middle position. Your porch light will blink on off, on off, on off. Now the ambulance can easily find the house with the blinking light. In addition, your neighbors will know that if they see your porch light blinking, you may be in trouble. Your neighbors would then come over to see if they could assist you while you wait for the ambulance. Isn't that an awesome idea?

If you were a sales rep for Del Webb and you pointed out why the outlets were higher, why there was a 3-position switch, and perhaps tossed in one other non-electrical item that adds value, could that help you in selling the house? Of course! Most sales people would love to have that arsenal of added value to pitch to their customers. The next question is "Would you sell the home at the same price as your competitors?" The answer is "No, you can charge more." The reason you can charge more is that you bring more value to the customer. The net result is that your close rate will go up and, with an increase in price, your margins will go up, too.

Another story: A builder of homes and apartments targeted the senior market. They built condos for seniors who wanted to purchase a place to live. They also built apartment complexes for those seniors who preferred to rent an apartment that was specifically built with senior citizens in mind. They did a great job of designing these living environments for seniors. Their website, however, was another story. Take a guess what size font was used? Ten point font. What would you guess was the age of the techie who designed the website? Clearly a twenty or thirty something, and obviously not a senior citizen.

Not only do you need to look at your business through the eyes of the customer; you also need to look at your business through the demographics of the customer. Think like a senior citizen and determine their possible problems or concerns. Applying that kind of focus to your job is critical to adding value to the demographic you serve.

CONSIDER GENDER

"TUFFER" THAN YOU THINK

Let's start with this pearl of wisdom. Women are different than men! How's that for rocket science?

Several years ago, I was invited to be the keynote speaker for Tuffy Muffler, a company that sells mufflers, brake jobs, etc. The attendees were franchise owners from various cities. Although the audience was predominantly male, there were several women in the audience. I also learned that approximately half of their customers are women.

I asked all the gentlemen to take their eyes off me and look at the ladies in the audience. The reason I wanted them to look at the ladies was that I was about to ask the women a question and I wanted the men to watch their response.

I asked the women, "As a customer buying a product, have you ever said or thought, 'I bet a man designed this product'?" The women erupted in laughter. Clearly, they identified with this issue. The men all had expressions on their faces that communicated, "What?"

Every woman in the audience knew exactly what I was referring to. The problem is that men don't have a clue how to design products for women. If your management team is predominately male and you are going to be marketing a product to women, perhaps you should interview the women in your company, or go home and interview your wife and your daughter. They have a much better shot at designing the play than you do.

I asked the women to pretend they were going on a field trip with me to visit a typical muffler shop. I asked them to describe what they thought the physical appearance of the facility would be like. They responded by saying:

- the waiting room was dirty;
- the bathroom was *disgusting*, and the seat was up;
- the magazines were all men's magazines, and some of them were more than two years old;
- the coffee must have been in the pot for several days—you could asphalt your driveway with that stuff;
- one woman said, "I wonder when they last washed that pot;"
- the couch had been torn and repaired with duct tape;
- the calendar was more "bikini babe" than calendar; and
- to top things off, the male employees all talked down to the female customers.

Almost all women can identify with this scenario. I asked the women to think about what they would do if they were going to open a muffler shop and their goal was to get a 100% share of the female market. Even though that goal might be unrealistic, the point of the exercise was to design a muffler shop by looking at it through the eyes of women. Their response was not rocket science:

- clean up the lobby;
- have spotless restrooms with a nice mirror, not a rectangular piece of aluminum;
- replace that couch with a new, attractive one and redesign the lobby so it looks attractive;
- clear out all the old magazines and include some magazines that women like to read;
- serve fresh Starbuck's coffee, tea and water;
- lose the calendar; and
- hire a female employee who will not talk down to female customers or try to "up-sell" them.

One of the men in my audience jumped all over this idea and decided to go home and interview his wife and daughter. Apparently his wife said, "You're really on to something. How about some toys for their kids to play with?"

The CEO of Tuffy Muffler invited me back the following year to speak at his conference. As the attendees were getting their coffee, he pointed to the same man. "That guy who was so excited after last year's conference—and guess what? –his business is up 43%."

The CEO then said, "See that other guy? Last year he told me, 'This is not a hospital; this is a dirty, greasy business,' and he has not implemented a single idea from last year's presentation. His business is flat."

It is interesting to me, after doing hundreds and hundreds of presentations, that there are always those who "get it" and there are always plenty who do not. This book is loaded with all kinds of ideas relative to adding value. Even though an example might not be from your specific industry, it doesn't mean the idea cannot be applied to your business. I often comment: "If you think I'm not talking about your business, you're correct. However, if you think I am talking about your business, you're also correct."

Michelle Neilson, founder and owner of Ms. Tuffy Auto Care Center, believes that vehicle maintenance and repair is something we all need to do, and that it should never be an intimidating or unpleasant experience for anyone.

Ms. Tuffy Auto Care Center is unique in the automotive repair industry in providing women of Richmond, Virginia with a place where they can take their vehicles for service while enjoying a luxurious and relaxing atmosphere. In addition to employing ASE Certified Technicians who are knowledgeable and trustworthy, additional services are offered that until now haven't been found at other shops or dealerships:

- Pick-up & Drop-off Service for Vehicle and Driver!

- Mall Shuttle

- Professional, Non-intimidating Service

- Easy To Understand Explanations of Your Vehicle

- Free Pre-travel Safety Checks for Ladies and Students

- Beautiful, Relaxing Atmosphere

- Wireless Internet Work Space

- Wednesday Spa Treatments

- Complimentary Vacuum Service with Your Visit

- Proudly Female Owned and Operated with Years of Automotive Experience.

VOLVO HAS 150 WOMEN DESIGN THEIR NEXT CAR

Volvo decided to take their female customers into consideration. They realized that a lot of women are buying cars and that their view of how to design a car might be different from men's. So Volvo organized a team of 150 women to design a concept car. They asked them to tackle some of the issues that women had with cars. One of the issues was that, with the advent of self-serve gas stations, the customer would frequently get petroleum fumes on their hands. The women really didn't want to go to work or to other events smelling like a refinery. So they engineered a gas cap more like the kind used on Formula One racecars. The gas nozzle goes in and out without having to remove the gas cap with your hands.

Then there was the issue of upholstery. Women know only too well that children get food, juice, candy, etc. on the car seats. They wanted the design to include removable seat covers so they could put them in the laundry. Oil changes were another big inconvenience. They decided they wanted to engineer a car that would need an oil change only every thirty thousand miles. In addition, they wanted a car where the woman owner would never have to go underneath the car or open the hood of the car. So they designed the car to be able to dial up the service provider when it needed an oil change or maintenance and schedule an appointment. Then the service provider would forward an email confirming the appointment. Parallel parking was another issue and they designed a technology to deal with it. When they pulled alongside a parking spot, the technology would measure the size of the opening to be sure it was big enough to park the car in. Then with the push of a button, the technology would take over and park the car for them!

CONSIDER DIVERSE MARKET SEGMENTS

In this next example the company has to consider more than one demographic. Whitsons Culinary Group prepares meals for a number of different market segments. Two of those segments are high schools and assisted-living residences. Is it safe to assume that the needs of the assisted-living market are going to be different than those of the high schools? Do senior citizens really want a steady diet of burritos, pizza, and burgers? What about portion size? Should they consider salt content and other ingredients? Too many companies have a one-size-fits-all mentality. Customers want products and services that are tailored to their specific needs, not yours. If an organization has diverse market segments like Whitsons Culinary Group, here's a tip on how to go about creating added value.

Tip: Have a meeting on Tuesday to brainstorm what the added value would look like to the assisted-living market. If possible, invite a few people in from that demographic. On Thursday, have another meeting to brainstorm what the added value would be for the high school demographic. All too often, companies discuss their added value in a single meeting. The outcome of this approach is that the organization comes up with a generic added value as opposed to added value ideas that are targeted specifically at their diverse market segments.

CONSIDER LOCATION

Inches vs. metric: Frequently when I speak, I am standing on a platform that could be eighteen inches or maybe twenty-four inches high. There are many manufacturers of stages that also manufacture the rolling carts for coffee, lunches, etc. I remember a gentleman who worked for one of these manufacturers. He came up to me after one of my presentations and said, "I think we are 'inside-out.'" He explained: "All of our catalogs show the dimensions of the stages in inches. However, we market to Europe." He then said with a grin, "Perhaps we should manufacture some of our products using the metric system." For companies that market to international markets, it is very easy to fall prey to doing everything in English and in inches. "Inside-out" again! This can be turned into an opportunity by transforming to "outside-in."

CONSIDER LANGUAGE

If you have a high percentage of clients where English is not their primary language, consider hiring somebody that speaks that language fluently. Gaftek is a company that installs and maintains gas tanks in the Northeast. A large percentage of their customers are convenience stores. Burnie Gaff, president of Gaftek, recently shared with me that he is considering hiring someone that speaks French for their northern operations and perhaps someone that speaks Hindi for some of their customers. He said he probably wouldn't get this done by the time this book goes to press since they are slammed with business right now. Consider the positive word-of-mouth possibilities when their customers get to talk to someone who speaks their native tongue.

During a customer focus workshop for Ivy Acres, several employees discussed the fact that English is not the first language of some of the retail customers of Home Depot, who is an Ivy Acres customer. However, all of the instructions listed on the plant tags for the bedding plants were written in English. The employees felt that writing the tags in both Spanish and English would add more value to the product. Ivy Acres now has instructions in Spanish.

Raymond Handling Solutions came to the same conclusion. Many of the operators that worked for their customers were Hispanic. However, the signs on the lifts they sold were all in English. Their employees decided to design signs in Spanish.

Apple Computer clearly designs their products for the eyes of "non-techies." If they looked at the business through the eyes of geeks, their products wouldn't come close to being as simple to use or have such a high "cool factor."

Apple is the poster child for "user-friendly." Most companies state that they want to be "easy to do business with"; however, they not only design their products from the "inside-out," but the majority of their processes are "inside-out" as well. There is no way they can be "easy to do business with" when all of their systems and processes are "inside-out."

Frequently, when I am doing a presentation and talking about Apple computers, participants will bring up the Apple Store, and how incredible their experience was. They comment about their experience when they bought a product. They ooze with enthusiasm when they share things like, "The salesperson stood right where the product was and swiped my credit card on her iPhone and asked me if I preferred to have the receipt emailed to me, printed, or both. Now we are talking "outside-in" and "easy to do business with." It's a reality, not just a statement. We need more companies like Apple.

In summary, everyone in your company should look at their business not only through the eyes of the customer, but also according to the demographics of that customer type. That could mean international customers, techies designing software for non-techies, age and gender as discussed above, and so on. Conducting focus groups with customers of specific demographics is an awesome idea.

Is your organization entirely focused on developing good customer relationships with a dose of schmoozing? Let me ask you, what are your competitors doing? Maybe it's time to get off "customer service" exclusively and drink the "customer focus" Kool-Aid.

Make Your Employee the Uncommon Denominator

I don't think much of a man who is not wiser today than he was yesterday. - **Abraham Lincoln**

Changing the Culture of a Company

When I was an executive I was transferred to corporate headquarters, where I called together all the employees from the various headquarters departments. They already knew that we were embarking on changing the culture of the company to one of becoming more customer focused.

I had the sense that many of the headquarters departments felt that becoming more customer focused was something that the various business units needed to focus on. I didn't get the sense, however, that they felt the culture needed to be integrated into the infrastructure of the company at the corporate level. After my intro on customer focus, I said, "All of the people in the field are customers of headquarters. Therefore, your jobs are to help them sell more, install more and support more. If you're not doing those things, then I'd like to know what you are doing on the payroll."

I also told them that headquarters was not the Gestapo. During my field visits, several sales reps said they felt that they had to be a buffer between the customer and headquarters. Some even indicated that they would never let anybody at headquarters talk to one of their customers for fear of alienating the customer. Others said that all calls from the customer had to go directly to the rep, to make sure that it would be handled properly. I replied that this would diminish their earnings; that we needed all departments to be assets to the sales team. If everyone was allowed to talk to customers, this would free up more time for the reps to sell. Consequently, revenue would go up and the commissions would go up with them.

When reps rely on their teammates to help in the appropriate areas, sales should climb. I did, however, want strict adherence to appropriate accounting, as well as the legal and ethical standards that were the core values of our company.

A COMPETITIVE ADVANTAGE STARTS AT THE TOP – WITH LEADERSHIP

Leadership, as a core competency, just might be the only true sustainable advantage. - Howard

A core competency that creates a competitive advantage is leadership. If the leadership skills of the management team are superior to the leadership skills of the competition, that would be a good start to winning in the marketplace. Everything emanates from great leadership. The problem is, we have far too many managers and not enough leaders. Employees in this country are starved for great leadership.

I have interacted with many senior executives of large corporations, and it's clear that most of them believe they are great leaders. My gut tells me—and this is backed up by employee comments—that less than 10% of executives today are great leaders.

EMPLOYEE VALUE ADDED

Economic Value Added (EVA) is a financial measure aimed at determining whether a company or organization has created shareholder value. Many companies use EVA as a measure of executive performance. In some cases, they also tie executive compensation to EVA. Therefore, it is safe to assume that organizations are keen on having their EVA increase.

One of my fundamental premises is that an increase in EVA is preceded by an increase in Customer Value Added (CVA). I don't know how you can get a high EVA unless the organization is passionate about creating substantial value for their customers. Having said that, I believe that CVA is preceded by Employee Value Added (another type of EVA).

Management's role is to focus on creating value for their employees by giving them the proper tools, training, technology systems, etc. This chapter will focus on many of the things that management needs to do to create Employee Value Added (EVA).

MAKING EMPLOYEES THE UNCOMMON DENOMINATOR

Employees will either be your competitive advantage or your competitive disadvantage. It's your choice! Too frequently, employees are hired and slam dunked into their job. Given no training and marginal opportunities for communication, employees are turned loose. You now have the inmates running the asylum. As a customer, have you ever heard, "I'm just new here." Translation, "I have no clue what I'm doing."

In that case, the employee has just become useless to the customer. What does the customer think when someone says "I'm just new here"? Customers get frustrated, as do the employees. Complaints rise and management blames the complaints on the employees. I recall a CEO who said to me, "We had a high number of customer complaints. I was frustrated, so I decided to add an incentive. The employees were incentivized to reduce the number of complaints. The number of complaints dropped dramatically." He indicated that he had "solved the problem."

But it isn't the number of complaints your company knows about that is the issue. It's the total number of complaints, and that includes the number of dissatisfied customers who never write a letter, call to express their dissatisfaction, or tell you directly that they are dissatisfied. His company reduced the number of complaints reported; however, the number of *silent dissatisfied customers*

31

probably increased. It's not the employee's behavior that needs to change; it is management's. Is it possible that management can be the company's competitive disadvantage? The employees spot that in a heartbeat.

Case Study: I'm confident that you can think of dozens of examples of poor behavior exhibited toward you when you were a customer. Ignoring the customer is one of those behaviors. Here is a classic example. The CEO of a company that hired us to do a workshop told me that he was recently at a store making a purchase. When he approached the clerk at the counter to pay for the product, he took out his credit card and handed it to her. At that moment, the phone rang. It was obviously a personal conversation. She was talking to a friend about what time they got off work. They were going to go shopping at the mall and perhaps go to the Olive Garden for dinner. She left him standing there while she continued the conversation, ignoring her customer.

He told me what he did, "I took out my cell phone and dialed the number of this store." When the receptionist answered, he asked to be transferred to this department. When her phone rang, she put her friend on hold and answered, saying "How can I help you?" He responded in a rather terse voice, "Turn around; this must be the only way I can get service around here." Is it fair to say that this employee might talk with her peers later and make the customer the problem? Is it likely she will take responsibility for her own behavior? This company will certainly get some WOM. It just won't be positive.

The question is, "Whose fault is it?" If you said the employee, I wouldn't make that your final answer. You may want to use your 50-50, or use a lifeline and call me because I know the answer. It's management's fault! If the employees in the organization are not doing the right stuff, it usually means management is not doing the right stuff. Management didn't communicate the play, nor did they provide appropriate training—perhaps they even hired the wrong person in the first place—and customer behaviors are not rewarded. This book outlines many steps regarding what management needs to do in order to help employees become the uncommon denominator. If management wants the employees' behavior to change, whose behavior needs to change first? If management doesn't change their behavior, what are the odds that employees will change theirs?

DUNN LUMBER

Dunn Lumber has multiple retail locations in the Pacific Northwest. They serve contractor employees as well as do-it-yourselfers. The management team realized that when their stores were busy, customer satisfaction was at its best. However, when the store was almost empty, service levels were at their lowest. When analyzing this scenario, they discovered that their employees were on the Internet, so when the next customer walked in they were invisible. The management and employees then drafted what they called "the not busy list."

Example is not the main thing in influencing others; it is the only thing. - *Albert Schweitzer*

When the employees were not busy, there was a list of things that they could be doing that would add value to other departments or the operation in general. They came up with two lists, one for the inside counter people and the second one for those that worked in the yard. Now employees had their list of things they could do that would make a positive contribution to the organization rather than wasting time cruising the Internet.

I recently heard a statistic that the average employee was spending from four to five hours a day either generating or reading emails. I couldn't help but wonder what percentage of those were related to their business and what percentage were personal. I don't know how any company can remain competitive when employees are spending that amount of time doing emails.

"Not Busy" List for Yard

_____ Level stacks
_____ Cover stacks
_____ Put away all incoming stock for yard/warehouse
_____ Sweep warehouses, yard areas, sidewalks & parking lots
_____ Pick up corners, stickers, trash
_____ Police the parking lot and landscape areas
_____ Empty trash cans
_____ Empty recycling containers
_____ Straighten finish and moldings
_____ Stock & cull finish and moldings (make adjustments)
_____ Stock MDF moldings (make adjustments)
_____ Stock BVG fir finish in office (make adjustments)
_____ Trim damaged ends on cedar boards and siding (make adjustments)
_____ Verify adequate ear/eye protection for all power saws
_____ Clean miscellaneous trash off the forklifts

_____Organize items in special order area, identifying possible dead items
_____Wash delivery trucks or forklifts
_____Vacuum and clean glass in delivery trucks
_____When above items are complete, contact a supervisor

"Not Busy" List for Sales

_____Stock shelves from incoming shipments or overstock
_____Face the merchandise outward
_____Empty garbage cans
_____Empty recycling containers
_____Make coffee, clean station, and stock supplies
_____Check for current signs and bar codes
_____Re-print damaged/faded signs
_____Replace torn plastic sign holders
_____Remove old staples from previous sign postings
_____Clean counters
_____Vacuum carpeted areas and rugs
_____Mop up coffee stains
_____Dust shelves and stock
_____Fill kids' wagon
_____Replenish literature at point of purchase
_____Clean glass in skylight, window and door displays
_____Address damaged inventory with supervisor in charge
_____Make sure all odd lot/dead items have signage
_____Address built up clutter on/around the counter area
_____Inventory office/sales supplies and promotional items
_____Identify stock-outs and research reason
_____Make sure restrooms are stocked and presentable
_____Address any safety issues
_____Follow up with customers on existing quotes
_____Stock moldings and finish lumber (make adjustments)
_____Cull moldings and finish lumber (make adjustments)

I can't help but wonder how many other companies could benefit from a "not busy" list. Is that dormant added value for your company?

I have discussed looking at the business through the eyes of the customer. Now let's shift gears and look at the business through the eyes of the employees. Years ago, numerous executives made the following statement: "The management team has a fire in their belly in terms of going the extra mile for the customer; why don't the employees have a fire in their belly?" The more I pondered this statement, the more I was determined to dig in and understand exactly why.

The Employee's Perspective

Whenever I do a workshop for a company, one of the questions I always ask the employees is: "What is the primary purpose of the business?" Without hesitation, the employees unanimously respond, "To make a profit." I respond affirmatively by saying, "That's correct. Let's put that on our list. However, let's put that on line number two." Then I ask the employees, "Why do you as employees want businesses to exist?" And the majority of them respond, "Because I need a job." Then I say, "Let's put 'create jobs' on line number three." I then say, "These two are both extremely important. No question about it. However, the key word was 'primary.' The *primary* purpose of the business is to create value for customers. Therefore, number one on our list will be: 'Create a customer.'"

Peter Drucker said the same thing, or very close:

1.   Create a customer;
2.   Make a profit;
3.   Create jobs.

You have to create something of value, so the customer will take out their checkbook, credit card, cash or purchase order and give you money in exchange for that product or service. If there is no value in the customer's mind, the business ceases to exist.

Creating Value Creates Jobs

The primary purpose of a business is to create a customer. - Howard

Then I say: "Now let's compare two companies in the same industry. Company A is five-star at creating value for the customer and company B is only one-star. In company A, what is going to happen to their ability to make a profit?" The employees respond, "It's going to go up." I ask: "Also, what is going to happen to their ability to create jobs?" The employees always respond, "It's going to go up." Then I ask: "And company B, where the value is only one star, as rated by their customers, what is going to happen to their ability to make a profit?" They respond, "It's going to go down." I ask: "And what is going to happen to that company's ability to create jobs?" The employees respond, "It's going to go down."

Now, here's the chicken and egg question: "What comes first, making a profit and increasing jobs for employees, or creating value for the customer?" The employees respond, "Creating value for the customer." Understanding the relationship between: 1) creating value for the customer; 2) profit; and 3) jobs is the first step in starting the fire in their belly for creating value for their customers.

CREATING FIRE IN YOUR EMPLOYEES THROUGH WIIFM

I am absolutely convinced that employees have 20/20 vision when they look at the business through their own eyes. Here's the challenge. If we go around the table and look at things through the customers' eyes, do our employees have that same 20/20 vision? Rarely.

COMPANY A	COMPANY B
Price based on VALUE	Price based on COSTS

Employees think "I gave up my lunch hour or stayed late to ship the product on time. I can see what's in it for the customer." My experience has also taught me that employees can see what's in it for the company if employees all work hard for the customer: the company makes more profit. However, the big question on the mind of all employees is, "What's in it for me?" Is it fair to say that all employees are tuned into radio station WIIFM? If the employees do not understand the relationship between creating value for the customer and WIIFM, then they have no gas in their tank to go the extra mile for the customer.

Mark Olson, president of APG, understands the WIIFM play. Mark called all of his employees together and said, "The economy is tough right now and our competitors think they're going to have a tough year. That is really good news for us. If we continue to bring more value to our customers, we'll persist in beating the competition and we'll have another good year." At that point, Mark called each employee to the front of the room and handed each one a $20 gas card redeemable at a local gas station in the area. He said to them, "I want to put some gas in your tank, in appreciation of you going the extra mile for the customer."

Mark called me later and said, "Howard, that $20 made a HUGE difference for people. They knew that their efforts were appreciated, and that their efforts made a difference in our ability to meet the customers' needs. The excitement around the company was incredible."

Would you agree or disagree with the following statement? "Employees in the United States feel underappreciated." There is no question about the answer. What would happen if they felt appreciated? Mark Olson "gets it." Unfortunately there are managers that don't. Perhaps they think, "We pay them a salary so they should just do their jobs." I'm sure many of Mark's competitors think that way.

I create a bucket called WIIFM and then say the following: "Let's assume that all employees in your company show up daily with the attitude, *I am here to be absolutely awesome at creating extraordinary value for my external and internal customers today.* In that case, what would be some of the WIIFMs that could happen now or down the road?"

Employees are very quick to come up with a very extensive list of WIIFM's. The short list usually includes: pay raise, bonus, tickets to a ballgame, gift certificate to a spa, time off, fun, a sense of teamwork and camaraderie, self-esteem, positive recognition from management and peers, promotions, job security, and a host of others.

Once they've established the list, I ask them, "Is that list sufficient justification to be dedicated to creating value for the customer and to go the extra mile?" The answer is a resounding "YES!"

The problem is that they have never been trained on this topic. Therefore, they have no understanding of the correlation between creating value for the customer and WIIFM. If employees have not connected the dots between "adding value" and "WIIFM," then they have no gas in their tank to go the extra mile for the customer! Whose fault is that?

One of the WIIFM's that always hits the list is "A raise." I always look at the employee who says, "A raise" and I say, "Let's pretend I'm your manager." To the rest of the group, I say, "He comes to me and says he needs a raise. His car is broken down, his rent is increasing, groceries are more expensive, and he needs more money." I then ask the employee, "Where do I get the capacity, not the authority, to give you a raise? Capacity and authority are two different things. Authority means: I am the boss; I sign a form and send it to Human Resources.

There is no traffic jam on the extra mile.

- Howard

Capacity refers to where the money is going to come from so that I can give some of it to you."

At this point, there is an absolutely blank stare on the face of all employees. And I say, "The money will not come from the boss, the President of the company, or anyone else. The money must come from your customers."

Macroeconomics by Howard:
The customer puts the money in,
the rest of us take it out.
End of Macroeconomics.

We not only take money out in terms of wages, but we also take money out in terms of supplies, materials, computers, etc.

The following awesome idea helped remind the employees of one company where their paychecks come from. They invited one of their top customers into the company on payday. Then they handed all of the paychecks to this customer. Employees came up single file to shake the hand of the customer, receive their checks, and say "thank you."

Another example of an awesome idea from one of our clients was the following. One of their employees was very artistic. They asked her to paint a mural on the wall of the employee lunchroom. She painted a mock employee paycheck in the center and then surrounded it with a series of different customer logos. Whenever a sales rep had a customer come into the facility, they usually took them to the employee cafeteria to get a cup of coffee. The sales reps used the wall as a marketing aid. They were quick to point out that the mural was on the wall as a constant reminder to all employees that they work for the customer. This was a two-fer, since it also reminded the employees where their paychecks and raises came from.

Every man should make up his mind that if he expects to succeed he must give an honest return for the other man's dollar.

- Edward H. Harriman

Sometimes I look at another employee and say, "Are you going to write a check to the company so that we can give this employee a raise?" You can guess the answer. I ask another employee to be the customer and I say, "We're late with the product, we don't return phone calls, we constantly say 'ship it…it's good enough,' we do it our way instead of your way, we do sloppy work, we never give you a heads-up when we are not going to make a delivery date." I say, "What are you going to do, as the customer?" She says, "I am going to find another supplier." I look at the employee that wants a raise and I say, "We're not talking a raise; we're talking a pay cut." *Why?* "We lost a customer. Not getting a raise or getting a pay cut might be the good news. Consider the alternative: we could lose our jobs."

An example I heard while doing a workshop was, "I can't see it from my house." They were talking about sloppy jobs some of their employees had done while installing high end appliances such as refrigerators, cooktops, etc. Their point was that even though the installers can't see sloppy work from their own houses after they leave the customer's, the customers are left to see it clearly every day. What type of WOM will this generate? Are these employees a competitive advantage? No, they're a serious disadvantage!

Looking back at the young lady who was playing the role of customer, I asked her, "What do I need to do if I want to get more money from you, the customer?" She responded, "You've got to get it to me on time; you've got to do it my way." Translation: "You have to think 'outside-in.' You have to listen to my needs and you have to create more value for me." I say, "Therefore, if I don't create any more value for you, you are not going to give me any more money, right?" She nods affirmatively. Now, I say to her, "Let's assume that we are absolutely awesome at creating value for the customer. Everything we do is 'outside-in.' We listen to your needs and respond to your inquiries on a timely basis. We are never late. We never make excuses. In other words, you think we are absolutely five-star at creating value for you. Now, what will you do?" She says, "I will tell others about you." Positive Word of Mouth. The customer is now your PWOM rep. The company is now getting referrals. Sales are growing. "Now you can get that raise."

Key Points for "Raise":
- Do not lose customers
- Add value for the customer
- PWOM = Referrals = Raise!

It is not the employer who pays the wages.
Employers only handle the money.
It is the customer who pays the wages.
- Henry Ford

The employee is now the competitive advantage. What type of WOM will be generated now?

Always do more than is required of you.
- George S. Patton

SIX STEPS TO GET YOUR EMPLOYEES TO BE "THE UNCOMMON DENOMINATOR"

I have always believed that the employees are the weapon. Many companies expound on this; however, it is rare that it is ever achieved. In today's highly competitive marketplace where Product Parity abounds, it is critical that all employees add value to the customer.

A powerful source of competitive advantage is the discretionary effort of your employees. Your employees can erode your competitive advantage by being indifferent to customers, driving them away as fast as your marketing efforts bring them in. Or, your employees can be empowered and energized to go on the offensive and use their discretionary effort to go the extra mile for the customer.

Here's one of the problems. In many organizations a customer walks in the door, there's a plaque on the wall that says "We're going to be number 1 in customer service" or "The customer is king," and yet, what the customer gets is something entirely different.

The employees have no clue they are the weapon. They have no clue that the plaque is referring to them. They have no idea their discretionary effort and ability to go the extra mile is what makes them the *uncommon denominator*. If they don't understand they are the weapon, then what are the odds they actually are?

When the espoused statements are not manifested by the employees' behaviors, including that of management, I refer to this as a "lack of congruence." It doesn't really matter what companies say; what matters to customers is how the company behaves. It's all about behavior.

Lack of Congruency

The challenge is how to get "alignment," so that the employees'—as well as management's—behaviors match the stated values.

Alignment

Example: A major hotel chain designed a brand-new marketing campaign to increase their share of business customers. Its tag line was, "Come stay with us, we guarantee no surprises." They spent hundreds of thousands of dollars on this campaign. However, when a customer showed up and got a surprise, they went to an employee and said, "What happened to 'no surprises?'" The employee's response was, "What do you mean?" It was very clear that the employees had no idea what this marketing campaign was all about. They weren't even told it was launched, let alone what they were supposed to do when a customer got a surprise.

This expensive campaign was immediately pulled. Frequently, management or marketing departments come up with these grandiose marketing statements. However, they forget the most critical part of the campaign, which is to ensure that all employees are on board and trained *before* the campaign is launched.

So, how can you increase your employees' discretionary effort? Let's go through the steps on how to get employees to be the *uncommon denominator*.

STEP 1: HIRE THE RIGHT STUFF

Too many companies simply run an ad, get many responses, bring in several responders, look at their resumes, their background, their qualifications, and make a bad hiring decision by hiring the tallest twerp. If you want your employees to be the uncommon denominator, you have to think beyond just technical skills or background. Let me give you some examples.

When Steve Jobs started a new division called "MacIntosh," he took a handful of his absolute best programmers. He told them that they had an incredible opportunity because the MacIntosh would change the world of computing forever, and they would be a part of this. He then told them that they would be responsible for interviewing all new hires for the MacIntosh division. Steve's instructions were that they had to make sure the new hires they selected were as talented and awesome as they were; they had to pick only the best. Can you imagine being interviewed individually by this panel? Are they going to hire the tallest twerp? The moral of the story is, "If you don't pick the best talent, then you are already one step behind, right out of the starting gate."

Barry Steinberg of Direct Tire and Auto Service in Massachusetts decided they didn't want to be an average tire dealer; they wanted to set themselves above the pack right from the start. So, rather than just run an ad and hire unemployed mechanics (i.e., get what their competitors were getting), this entrepreneur actually went to a headhunter—that's right, a headhunter to recruit mechanics. They talked about the requirements of the job and what skills were needed. They didn't want somebody who'd been hopping from job to job every three or four months. They spelled out the specific requirements of what makes a great mechanic. With this information, the headhunter recruited great mechanics.

Next, Direct Tire and Auto Service interviewed all prospective employees three times. The first interview was at 7 am, to see if they were punctual and alert. The second one was at the end of the day, to make sure there were no mood swings or change in energy level. The third, if they made the cut, was at midday with their potential supervisor.

Is there any doubt in your mind that in this case, the employee is the uncommon denominator? They don't just claim to have great mechanics; they actually do. They took the right steps to make sure their new employees were the uncommon denominator by hiring the right raw clay in the first place.

There is a saying in the training business: "If you give us monkeys, we'll give you back trained monkeys," meaning, you can't do much with the wrong raw clay. Sure you can educate them, but they will never give you the results you are looking for. If you want to play the game at the awesome level, you have to hire warm, friendly, nice people. Don't hire people with a burr under their saddle or people that everybody refers to as having an attitude. Begin by hiring the "right stuff."

Average: Run a classified ad and hire the tallest twerp.

Awesome: Have your best employees interview candidates.

Awesome: Use headhunters to hire mechanics.

One of management's roles is to "weed the garden." If management doesn't weed the garden, let me ask you, "Who is in jeopardy of leaving your company? Would it be your weak performers or your top performers?" The best way to lose your top performers is to not weed the garden.

What happens to the performance of your key employees if you do not weed the garden? When you finally weed the garden, what do your employees say? "Well, Howard, what took you so long? We figured it out ten months ago." When you weed the garden, what happens to the performance of the team? It goes up. My experience, from doing hundreds of workshops for companies that are in the higher end of their industry, shows that a majority of employees in those companies realize that their company needs to "weed the garden."

Another one of management's key roles is to eliminate negative attitudes. Employees and managers with negative attitudes are a cancer that "metastasizes" throughout your organization. When I ran businesses, I communicated that one of my absolute top pet peeves was a negative attitude. I told all employees that if I ever caught someone with a negative attitude, I would write a letter of recommendation for them. I said, "Don't worry; it will be a great positive letter." Then I would take that employee in my car and drive them straight to the competition for their interview. They would become our secret weapon.

43

If there are employees in the organization who have a negative attitude, whose behavior needs to change? If you answered "the employee," I wouldn't make that your final answer. Management's behavior needs to change. Management is tolerating the negative attitude. It's your fault, coach!

Think Outside of the Box
in Terms of Finding Awesome Employees.
Average Recruiting
Results in Hiring Average Employees.

Hire the best, weed out the rest. - Howard

Example 1: At the end of the first day of a workshop, I told the participants that some of us would have the opportunity to be a customer this very evening. I said, "I will eat dinner at the restaurant of the hotel. Some of you may go to the Apple Store or pick up your dry cleaning, etc. If you are in the position of being a customer this evening, keep your eyes open for a great moment in customer focus. Also, look for a not so great moment in customer focus. We will have two or three of you share your examples in the morning."

You get what you tolerate. - Howard

Geff Yancey was CEO of the company and he had expressed his frustration about how difficult it was to find truly great employees. When Geff shared his experience on the morning of the second day he said, "The young man that mows my lawn does an awesome job." Then he shared an example of what this young man had done recently. Geff said, "This young man looks at the weather on the Internet, and if any storms are in the forecast, he will double up the number of lawns that he does on say, the Wednesday or Thursday before the weekend. He has a hard hat that he has duct taped a flashlight to. He neatly writes a note for the customer, 'Dear Mr. Yancey, I noticed in the forecast that there was going to be thunderstorms on Friday evening and I wouldn't have been able to mow your lawn. Therefore, I doubled up my schedule on Wednesday and Thursday so that you could have a nice lawn for the weekend. Have a great weekend,' and he signed his name."

I looked at Geff and said, "Did you hire this guy for your company?" All too often we run ads in the local classifieds to find employees when awesome employees are right under our noses. A work ethic like this is hard to train. This person's parents and grandparents have already done an outstanding job of training this individual. It is easier to train employees regarding your business than it is to train what this young man has already displayed.

Example 2: Another awesome example is Duncan Moffat, President of Data Aire, Inc. We had done several workshops for his company and I was returning to do another. When I approached the front door of the company, I noticed a huge sign on the front lawn. The sign was several feet long and several feet high and it read "Now Hiring." I mentioned to Duncan, "Business must be good; I noticed the sign on the front lawn." Smiling, he responded affirmatively. He then shared with me, "When we run an ad in the local paper's classified section, the quality is marginal at best. However, the quality of the applicants that we're getting from the sign is very high."

Who is responding to the sign? Employees who are working down the street. He commented, "A president of a company down the street sent his administrative assistant down to see what type of positions we are recruiting for. Perhaps he's trying to shore up and not lose some of his key employees." The point is that there are awesome people that you can run into when you go to Home Depot, the local restaurant, etc., or perhaps down the street. You, as well as your managers and other employees, should keep your eyes open for these outstanding individuals. Get their names and phone numbers so that you have a contact list of awesome talent when you need it. On the other hand, maybe it's time to weed the garden and replace a mediocre employee with someone on your awesome list. Another great source of awesome talent is asking your current employees. Birds of a feather flock together. They may have friends in their network that are awesome.

Tip: Be on the lookout for awesome employees when either you or your team is in the role of customer and build a contact list.

STEP 2: COMMUNICATION

You must communicate, communicate again, and then communicate some more . . . . Communicate, communicate, communicate . . . pretend I said communicate a hundred times.

Communication is the glue that holds it all together. When you are tired of hearing yourself say "the customer is number 1" or whatever your mantra is, and after you've said it over, and over, and over again, don't stop. Resist the temptation to stop because, let me tell you, this is when it's just beginning to take hold. In other words, you can't just say it once; that would be analogous to asking your son or daughter to clean their room just once. It isn't going to work. The more you realize the employees are the uncommon denominator, the more you will realize how critical it is to "frequently communicate" with them. I believe that an organization cannot attain world-class quality and world-class customer focus without *world-class communication*.

What do we need to communicate to our employees?

EMPLOYEES OFTEN DON'T KNOW THEY ARE THE UNCOMMON DENOMINATOR

The employees must know that they are the difference, if, in fact, they are going to execute the play and be the uncommon denominator. The discretionary effort of employees is a tremendous source of competitive advantage.

The discretionary effort of employees is a tremendous source of competitive advantage. - Howard

Inside of every human being is the capacity to go the extra mile for the customer. At the employee's discretion, they choose to let it out, or not. "It's not my job," or "the computer won't let me," or "I'll have to check with the manager," are all excuses. It's the stuff that comes out of an employee's mouth when they don't want to go the extra mile. If employees understand that they are the uncommon denominator, they will be more likely to choose the extra mile. Then the customer wins and so does everyone else.

The following example indicates poor communication with employees. What would happen if you walked into a room full of employees and asked them to write down the answer to the question, "What is our company's unique competitive advantage?" Give them a few moments to write out their answer. Now, let me ask the question, "What are the odds they wrote basically the same answer?" Not good. Most employees have very different ideas about what sets their company apart from the competition.

Who is going to execute the company's competitive advantage? The employees! So, what happens when the employees need to execute the play, but they don't know what the play is? I would like to challenge you with this question: How well do your employees know the play?

Rate Your Communication With Employees:

A   B   C   D   E   F

Maybe the real test would be to ask employees to grade your company's communication effectiveness. Then compare management's ratings with the employees' ratings.

Here is another example where poor communication with employees is obvious. On one occasion, the President of the company said to me, "Our company just did a customer satisfaction survey 60 days ago." I then asked the employees, "What were the top three or four things your organization was rated highest on, and what were the things your organization was rated weakest on?"

As is often the case, the response was: "deer in the headlights." Yet who is going to improve the performance on those items that need improvement? The employees! They can't do that if they don't know what to improve. The company knows what has to be improved, but they don't tell the employees! Also, it was clear, and most unfortunate, that no positive recognition had been given in those areas where they had scored high. In this case, the survey could have been an effective tool to drive change, but it hadn't been used to advantage.

Tip:
- When you conduct a survey, communicate the results to all employees, highlighting the areas where the company excelled. Give kudos for the successes. Also note the areas where the company was rated weaker.
- Select and discuss those areas that are targets for improvement.
- Assign a specific employee to each area where the company needs improvement. Give them the responsibility to brainstorm with coworkers on how best to improve the company's performance on that item.

First, we have to communicate to our employees that they are the uncommon denominator; then they can become the company's competitive advantage.

Top of mind awareness is a term that marketing people use to measure how

When all is said and done, more is said than done. - Lou Holtz

aware people are of a product or a brand. If a group of people were asked to write down the two top soft drink manufacturers in the world, what would they write? Probably Coke & Pepsi. If 90% of the people wrote Pepsi, Pepsi would have 90% top of mind awareness. If 100% wrote Coke, Coke would have 100% top of mind awareness.

If you have ever bought a brand-new car, what is the first thing you notice? That model of car suddenly seems to be everywhere. Obviously they didn't manufacture and sell all those cars last week. Something has happened that triggers your mind to recognize that car.

All too often, the top of mind awareness of employees on customer focus is low. Employees constantly walk by opportunities where they could add value but they don't see them. Very few employees come by this naturally unless their parents and grandparents did an exceptional job of training them. Without training, employees can walk by opportunities to add value and never see them. That is not the case at Westrec Marinas. The following is a letter sent by a customer of one of their marinas.

Hi Sherri,

I store my boat on the trailer in space 225. I am very inexperienced at boating. My wife couldn't back a trailer down any ramp, so it is actually hard for me to launch the boat when I want to use it. It is great that the staff at Tower Park will launch the boat for me and that is the reason that I chose Tower Park for my boating. I think my boat has been there for about two years. I do not use the boat that often. Last year it was only launched once on the Labor Day weekend. I live far away from the marina so sometimes it is not simple for me to come and tend to the boat. Last year I left the drain plug in the boat and could not make it to the marina to take it out before the rain came. I was afraid that when I arrived my boat would be a bowl full of water but Jack had turned the boat around (bow up) and taken the plug out for me. I don't worry about my boat being far away because I know more eyes are on it than mine. During launching and taking my boat back out of the water, Jack is always willing to go the extra distance, such as times when I don't think the boat is on the trailer just right. He helps me to have a great boating experience.

That is the reason that I chose Tower Park for my boating.

This past weekend my wife, granddaughter and I decided that we wanted to go boating. I had pulled the boat home a month ago to clean it and service it for this season. I pulled it back to Tower Park and had it launched. Who wants to sleep in a little cabin the size of Superman's phone booth when you can have the comfort of Motel 6? I guess if you are really into boating you have to do the cuddy thing and we did that night. After about an hour in the boat, the security guard, Allen, came knocking on the boat because my granddaughter had left my wife's purse on the outside seat. He also stated that it looked like the boat was taking on water. I looked into the bilge and didn't see any water but then I was paranoid, so I watched the bilge all night. No water. The next day it was very windy so instead of taking the boat out in the morning we decided to take a trip to San Francisco. When we returned to the boat, the ice chest was floating in the cabin of the boat! The boat was sinking.

Jack and Allen are not just employees of Tower Park Marina; they are very experienced employees that are used to working around boats. It is this experience that makes up for the inexperience of all of those like myself. (There are actually others that don't know the difference between forward and reverse.) If I need fuel, Jack will show me how to put it in the boat. Allen is constantly making the rounds, so my boat is safe not only in the fenced area but also at the dock. These guys are going to make sure that we always have a great boating experience. Because of economic hard times, we were thinking about giving up our space at Tower Park, but because we have discovered that Tower Park gives us so much more than just launching and storing our boat, we are going to stay there and don't see any future plans for change.

Jack and Allen deserve some employee recognition. It was late when we left the marina and I didn't get to personally thank Allen. Please tell him for me that the guy with the little boat in space 225 appreciates him looking out for us when we are at Tower Park. Scott

Is there any doubt that the employees at Tower Park Marina have high top-of-mind awareness in terms of Customer Focus? Employees in so many companies walk by these kinds of opportunities all the time. They never see them…but this is not the case at Westrec.

EMPLOYEES OFTEN DON'T KNOW WHAT THEIR MISSION STATEMENT MEANS

Many companies have a mission statement or vision statement and a list of values. They are documented, and perhaps they are even on a plaque on the wall. Management spends a great deal of time and energy creating these statements; then, they forget to communicate the meaning to their employees. Employees tend to be passive; they wait for management to come along and explain what the big picture is all about.

You see, the employees need to know what the mission statement means relative to their particular department. To a shipping clerk, does it mean, "I stay after and make sure the product gets out on time"? To an accounting employee, does it mean, "I make accurate and clear invoices"? If management does not communicate the meaning to the employees at each specific level, then I'm going to suggest that the employees don't know the play.

I was scheduled to deliver a speech to the US Postal Service. I found out the senior management team had gone off-site and had come up with an incredible vision statement. So, I said, "Send me a copy!" I held it up several times during my presentation. When I talked about various examples, I held it up and said, "This is what we're talking about, your vision statement. This is how you bring it alive."

When I finished my presentation, the senior executive asked the group, "How many of you remember when we went off-site a couple of years ago to brainstorm our Vision Statement?" Every hand went up. "How many were very excited about the really great job we had done in coming up with just the right words to put in the statement?" All hands went up. "How many of you have a plaque on the wall of your office with this vision statement?" All hands went up. He said, "I just made an observation. I think that Howard has just referenced our vision statement, in his presentation, more often than we have collectively talked about it ourselves. How many agree with that statement?" All hands went up. He then said, "We either need to take those plaques down or start talking about how to make the things on that plaque a reality in our various departments. How many think that would be a good idea?" All hands went up.

Often companies craft vision statements, mission statements, marketing slogans and so on. However, the reality is, the statements never get any legs in the organization. Nothing is done to make those statements come alive.

I have been impressed with the urgency of doing. Knowing is not enough; we must apply. Being willing is not enough; we must do. - Leonardo da Vinci

As much as we have to communicate to our employees what the mission/ vision statement of the company means, we also have to communicate what it means to each particular department.

STEP 3: TRAINING

So now you've hired the "right stuff." You've communicated to the employees what your unique competitive advantage is, what your mission statement is, and that they are the uncommon denominator. The next step is to provide training.

Everybody knows that the Ritz Carlton excels at customer service. Let me ask you a question: Do the employees at Ritz Carlton understand that they are the weapon; that they are the uncommon denominator? They are what set the Ritz apart from the average.

Does Ritz Carlton train their employees? Is there any question? When I interviewed several Ritz Carlton employees, I asked about how management gets the employees to do all this incredible stuff? One of the responses was, "Training, training, training." One of the valets told me that he had received three days of training on how to park a car.

I said, "You mean to tell me if Ritz Carlton hired me, and I already knew how to park a car, that I would have to go through three days of training?" The young man said, "But you don't know how to park a car the Ritz Carlton way." I said, "What is unique about parking a car at the Ritz Carlton?" He said, "You don't just park a car anywhere; you have to find out if the customer is going to use the car soon, this afternoon, or in a couple of hours. If so, we're going to park it toward the front end of the parking lot. If they are not going to use it for a couple of days, then we can put the car further in the back."

You see, they designed a system where they park the car so that they can get the car back to the customer quicker. That's but one small example of the level of detail in the training that Ritz gives their employees. Think about it…

three days of training on how to park a car. How many days of training do your employees get?

Here's an interesting question. Is training an expense or is it an investment? I'm going to suggest that all the organizations that have a short term culture, or are focused on the bottom line results this month, view training as an expense. I'm also going to suggest that the long term thinkers—the Ritz Carlton, Raymond Handling, Apple Computer, Sandhill Scientific, etc.—view training as an investment. It is an investment in their human capital; it is an investment in their competitive advantage.

Here is a multiple choice scenario:

a) Train employees and take the risk they quit. In other
   words, should we spend the money?
b) Not train them and take the risk they stay.

THE COST OF NOT TRAINING

"I feel your pain." A series of mistakes created a real problem for a Sandhill customer. Sometimes it is hard for an employee to truly understand how their behavior can impact a customer—either positively or negatively. But there are ways to drive the lesson home. In Sandhill's case, one product the company sells is a medical device that records patient information as part of a 24-hour diagnostic test (the patient undergoing the diagnostic procedure wears a small recorder during the 24-hour test period). Due to a technical problem, the hospital couldn't download the data, so they sent the recorder back to Sandhill via FedEx.

Unfortunately, a series of mistakes were made by one of Sandhill's service technicians, a young lady we'll call Patty. While Patty was able to download the patient data, she forgot to fax it back to the hospital. More importantly, she forgot to return the recorder. Of course, the hospital had scheduled additional patients—patients that had to be sent home when the recorder didn't arrive. The hospital called Patty, who provided an apology and said she'd get the recorder out "right away." Patty added "send the recorder back" to her to-do list. But by the end of the day, Patty hadn't made it this far down her list, so the recorder sat in the service department. Again, the hospital had to send patients home. They called Sandhill a third time, and Patty decided to take the recorder straight to the shipping department without delay. However, she did not tell Sandhill's shipping department to return the recorder via FedEx. Instead, the recorder was returned using regular mail (and there's a reason it's referred to as "snail mail"!) More delays, more patients sent home. To resolve this new delay, Sandhill did FedEx a second, "loaner" recorder once the hospital had called for the fourth time!

Patty explained the reasons for the delays, but management felt Patty did not really recognize how something like this impacts the customer. They decided NOT to say anything about it to Patty at this time. They did decide, however, to educate Patty.

Payday arrived and there was no paycheck for Patty. Instead, Patty's supervisor was told to hand her a note saying: "We left off some information the payroll agency needs to get your check done. We're fixing it and you should get your check in a week or two." Patty was understandably upset and ended up in the CEO's office complaining, "Not getting my check is unacceptable . . . I have a mortgage payment that's due . . . I have to have the check on time . . . It's the company's obligation to pay me on time and I shouldn't have to suffer because of a mistake the company made!"

This, of course, opened the door to her training session. It was clearly pointed out that a customer not getting their recorder back was unacceptable...that the hospital had patients to serve . . . that it was Sandhill's obligation to return the recorder. The hospital and their patients shouldn't have to suffer because of a mistake Sandhill made. In effect, the recorder was just as valuable and important to the hospital as Patty's paycheck was to Patty. The CEO reached into his desk and handed Patty her paycheck.

The message was heard, and felt, and remembered. From that moment on, not one item to be returned to a customer has been delayed.

STEP 4: THE RIGHT TOOLS

You've got to give your employees the right tools. If we go back to the Direct Tire Company, they recruited the best mechanics through a headhunter, and then they invested in the best equipment. Give employees "the best tools." Just think of the impact on them. It will positively affect their psyche and the quality of the work they do. When you give better-than-average employees the best equipment, they can perform their functions better than anybody else.

A casino in Las Vegas supplies their staff with smart phones. They use RFID chip technology on their customer loyalty cards. When one of their "premier" members walks through the door, a message is sent directly to the phone with the member's name and photo. The staff can then greet the member and expedite the check-in process. The tool—in this case the RFID chip—is the "enabler" that allows the employees to add value.

STEP 5: EMPOWERMENT

Empowerment is one of the critical steps to developing a powerful team. Empowerment has been bantered about for years. However, the employees are too often unsure of how far they can go; whether it's safe to make decisions.

You've hired the "right stuff," you've communicated the play, and you've provided the appropriate training. The next step is empowerment. What does empowerment mean?

Take note: I firmly believe that the training step must precede the empowerment step. That's the correct order. If you do it the other way around, then you might have the inmates running the asylum.

I really believe that if managers let go of the small stuff, they'll gain control of the most important issue, which is the competitive advantage. Too frequently, managers micromanage and make every decision for the employee. I call that the "Bubba School of Management." Check your brains at the door; bring all the problems to me; I'll solve them; I'll let you know what the play is. Employees are far more capable of making decisions than management sometimes gives them credit for.

I like to think management's role is to create the environment that will allow the employees to execute the play. Management needs to think strategically and make strategic decisions. Let the employees make the day-to-day tactical decisions. In my opinion, at this stage, the best thing management can do is simply get out of the way.

The employees must be viewed as a critical part of your competitive advantage and they must be treated as such. Ritz Carlton has as one of their guiding principles: "Our customers are ladies and gentlemen being served by ladies and gentlemen."

Management needs to get out of the way. - Howard

Ritz Carlton empowers their employees. Every Ritz Carlton employee has a $2,000 bucket of money. I don't literally mean a bucket with bills hanging out of it. It's an account with $2,000 dollars in it. Every Ritz Carlton employee gets $2,000 per year. Whatever they need to do "to knock the socks off the customer," they have the money to do it. When I asked several Ritz Carlton employees how much of that $2,000 they usually spent on a customer, most of them pondered the question and looked up at the ceiling to think for a few minutes. Then answers like $50, $75, or $125 would come out. The point is, the Ritz has taken the handcuffs off their employees.

Let's take a look at an example where a decision needs to be made to solve a problem. In Scenario A, the employees solve the problem. In Scenario B, the employees bring the problem to the manager and the manager solves the problem. Let's discuss the ramifications of these two decisions.

First, which scenario, A or B, are the employees more likely to implement? The answer is A. Why? Because they have "bought into" the solution. They came up with it. They are invested in it. Therefore, they are more likely to implement it.

Second, which is probably the better solution, the employee's or the manager's? The employee's solution is. Why? Because they are closer to the problem; they are intimately involved with it. Therefore, it is more likely that they came up with a higher quality solution than the manager did.

Third, if the employees need to keep checking with the boss, it slows everything down. All too often, organizations become lethargic because of a chain of command where too many approvals are needed before a decision is made.

I'm not sure Jack said "gluteus maximus," but we'll use it. I'm sure you get the visual.

This means the decision is delayed, and that can result in higher expenditures and slower response time. The employees get frustrated and it can certainly impact customer satisfaction. Customers are waiting for answers or decisions and the longer

If you have your eyes looking up at the boss, then the boss is the customer and you have your gluteus maximus pointed toward the customer.
- Jack Welch, Retired Chairman & CEO, GE

they wait, the less impressive your organization is. This will start up the NWOM machine. Supervisors and managers need to let go and let the employees make the tactical decisions. This will increase the speed of the decision-making process.

You will miss 100% of the shots that you do not take. - Wayne Gretzky

There are numerous small decisions that come up and if the employee is not empowered to take those shots, the opportunity is lost.

Fourth, think about employee morale. What happens when they are not allowed to make decisions and they always have to run to the boss to ask for permission? By empowering them with the minor decisions, the employees will feel much better about themselves and their team.

It is clear that empowering your employees is a great competitive advantage; so how do you make that happen? The following five steps come from observing companies in terms of where empowerment works and where it does not. If you don't do at least the first two steps, it's not going to work! You can't just walk into a group of employees and say, "You're all empowered now!" What does that mean to the employees? It means nothing. Here's what you have to do to make empowerment work.

KEY POINTS OF EMPOWERMENT

EXPLAIN:
You must explain empowerment based on the employee's function in the company. It will mean different things to a sales rep, a bookkeeper, a programmer, etc. For example, a sales rep may have empowerment boundaries having to do with pricing or discounts; they may have some capabilities in regard to committing to rush jobs. Accounting folks may be allowed to make financial decisions or authorize petty cash. In other words, you must explain empowerment in the vocabulary or vernacular of each person's function in the company. Each person needs to be very clear about exactly what types of decisions they are allowed to make.

BOUNDARIES:
You must draw a line in the sand—how far can the employee go? A sales rep's line, for example, may be, "You can give up to a 10% discount." The limit needs to be very clear. In terms of committing to early delivery of a product, the boundaries must also be clear. "You can tell the customer they will get the

product early, but no more than three days early." An accounting person's line, for example, may be, "You can authorize up to $50 of petty cash." Again, the boundary line is clear. These are decisions the employees can make without asking for permission. If they don't know where the line is, then they don't know how far they can go; they don't know if it is safe.

It's important for employees to know that it is safe to stick their neck out. I call this the "Turtle School of Management." Supervisors and managers need to make it safe for an employee to make some decisions. Without empowerment, we are not tapping into the full capabilities of our employees.. Often, employees feel stymied because they are not allowed to make simple decisions.

It's awfully difficult to steal second base
if you keep your foot firmly planted on first base.
- Author Unknown

Let's take a cue from Nordstrom regarding empowerment. Nordstrom has an employee handbook. It's a card about 5 X 8 inches.

Welcome to Nordstrom

We're glad to have you with our Company. Our number one goal is to provide outstanding customer service. Set both your personal and professional goals high. We have great confidence in your ability to achieve them.

Nordstrom Rules: Rule #1: Use best judgment in all situations. There will be no additional rules.

Please feel free to ask your department manager, store manager, or division general manager any question at any time.

These employees don't have to run to the manager with "Mother, may I?" every ten seconds to get permission to do something. The employee is empowered by this rule: "Use best judgment in all situations."

How many of you remember the Apple Computer ad several years ago that indicated that anybody—anybody on the plant floor—has the authority to shut

The only time a turtle makes progress is when it sticks its neck out. - Howard

down the entire line, and it happens. That's putting your money where your mouth is. That's walking your talk in the eyes of the employees.

ASK:

If you are wondering about what type of decisions the employees should be allowed to make, one of the easiest ways to find out is to ask the employees. Ask the employees in a department who perform a particular function: "What type of decisions do you feel you should be making?" That can be a great conversation. Employees know where the roadblocks are and what slows the process down. Sometimes employees can make managers and supervisors aware of roadblocks they didn't even realize existed.

ALLOW:

Resist the temptation to make decisions that you know the answer to. Often, a newly promoted supervisor or manager was an employee who performed very well in a technical function or skill, before the promotion. Now an employee brings a decision to that supervisor and because he has the technical expertise to understand the situation, he makes the decision. This can be one of the biggest mistakes a supervisor or manager can make. What are you training this employee to do? To bring all decisions to you. Let the employee know that he or she can make that decision. Even if you know the answer, it may be far more important to give that decision back to the employee, if that decision is clearly within the boundaries of the empowerment you have spelled out. If you push that decision back on the employee, they will soon learn what is within their boundaries and that your expectations are that they are capable of making those decisions. Too often, a supervisor will just react to the question. They don't think about whether their behavior will encourage empowerment or take it away.

REWARD:

Celebrate the small stuff. Celebrate the successful decisions. Too often, management waits until the end of the project or the end of the year to celebrate profit, etc. If you think about sports teams, they always celebrate the small stuff. Don't wait until the end of the game to celebrate. Do sports teams celebrate a hit, celebrate a defensive play, celebrate a home run, celebrate a first down, celebrate a great catch? Of course they do. The same thing applies in the business world. If you want to encourage the empowerment of all employees, one of the keys will be to give recognition, in front of their peers, to employees who stick their neck out and make a decision.

It may also be key to celebrate a decision that did not work out. Why? If an organization never makes a mistake, then they are not taking enough risks.

Obviously we do not want to be lackadaisical and create a lot of mistakes. However, risk taking and pushing the edge of the envelope is an important competitive advantage in many organizations.

Babe Ruth set the record for the most home runs in a season, but he also held the record for the most strikeouts. Lesson: You're not going to hit a home run every time, but you must be willing to take the risk and try.

If an organization never makes a mistake,
then they are not taking enough risks. - Howard.

POSITIVE REINFORCEMENT WORKS BETTER THAN NEGATIVE

Management needs to focus on rewarding the behaviors they espouse. Dr. W. Edwards Deming, who was one of the world's leading quality gurus, stated, "The American propensity for negative performance appraisals is the number one management problem."

I could not agree more. Turn the clock back to when we were in elementary school. Think about the following scenario when the teacher had us play "what's wrong with this picture?" What Ed was talking about was that when something happens, when the quality isn't right, or there is a customer complaint, we have a tendency to shoot the messenger. Managers dump on the employee in a negative way. They act like it's the employee's fault. "Why can't you get it right?" If managers act in a negative way, will the employee bring them another problem next week? Not a chance. Even though employees know where the problems are, and they know where the cracks are, they won't stick up their hand and take the risk of reporting them. Why be the messenger who gets shot? The result is: management thinks there aren't any customer complaints or internal problems. Management has solved the problem! Has management really solved the problem? No . . . they *are* the problem!

Another consideration is this: If management blasts the employees every time something goes wrong, the employees will probably not retaliate; instead, they will bottle up their frustration and anger. Then when they are confronted with an angry customer, they will probably vent their frustration on the customer.

COUNTERINTUITIVE THINKING

The process is the problem, not the employees. It may be counterintuitive to act in a positive manner when there is a problem, a mistake or a customer complaint, but it is actually the right management behavior.

Management is doing the wrong things. - Howard

Think for a moment about how you train a dog. Do you beat it with a stick when it doesn't do what you want, or do you give it a biscuit or a treat when it does the right thing? Management needs to think more about their behavior if the employees are doing the wrong stuff. If the employees are doing the wrong things, it's usually because management is doing the wrong things. Whose behavior needs to change?

A better response to an employee who brings the manager a problem might be, "I am glad we've got people like you who really care about the customer and who care about the company. I understand we've got this problem. What do you think we ought to do about it?" In other words, we must act in a more positive way. More support for employees can result in eliminating policies, procedures and structures that inhibit employee involvement and flexibility.

When we were trying to find out how you get the employees' behavior to match senior management's vision, we did some research on behavior change. We did a lot of reading in the social journals, the psychology journals, and the organizational development journals. We were looking for the sophisticated stuff. The problem is, it isn't sophisticated . . . it's sandbox. I noticed that these experts were talking about using positive KITAs to change behavior more than negative KITAs. A positive KITA stands for a positive "kick in the gluteus maximus." In other words, a positive kick in the pants (positive reinforcement) will change behavior more than a negative kick in the pants. Leaders need to resist the temptation to give negative feedback. Here's the choice: "Do you stroke 'em, or do you choke 'em?"

The American propensity for negative performance appraisals is the number one management problem. - Dr. W. Edwards Deming

After I shared this with a CEO, he told me, "I returned from vacation two weeks ago. I must have blasted ten employees (negative KITAs) and complimented only one (positive KITA)." He then said, "My *stroke 'em to choke 'em* ratio is out of kilter." He realized that it was his behavior that needed to change.

Tip: For the next week, keep a log with two columns. One with a "+" sign and one with a "–" sign. Now, keep track of how many positive KITAs you passed out and how many negative KITAs you passed out. This is a great tool to show what your stroke 'em to choke 'em ratio is.

In *The One Minute Manager*, Ken Blanchard used the phrase, "Catch them doing something right." I've taken it a step further. As another helpful tool, in many organizations I have simply suggested that management make "Catch the Employees Doing Something Right" sheets. You can fit four of these on one piece of paper (they turn out to be the size of a telephone message pad.) Print the words, "Catch the Employees Doing Something Right," and then draw a smiley face four times on the page. Underneath those four headlines, put four blank lines with checkmarks next to them. The goal is to find four employees that are continuously improving, creating more value for the customer and/or going the extra mile. Go catch four employees this week, and give them a pat on the back; a positive KITA. Take that little piece of paper and put it in your appointment book or iPhone every Monday morning. Start the week with a personal goal of

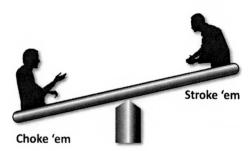

ADD VALUE OR STAY HOME

finding four people that are doing the right stuff relative to quality, customer focus or whatever you are trying to pursue in your particular organization.

Positive reinforcement is one of the tools that management needs to use in order to get the employees to be the uncommon denominators. The key is to reward the desired behavior. Decide what you want the employees to do, then reward that. The typical American employee feels under-appreciated. Do you agree or disagree with this statement?

The next question is: Whose job is it to make them feel appreciated? Management shouldn't be so busy making decisions that they don't stop and say, "Thank you." Say, "I appreciate you going the extra mile." It's important to take the time to stop and pat them on the back. The return from a small gesture like this will be larger than you might expect.

In one organization, where we trained all the employees, I called the CEO after the training, and the receptionist said, "Mr. Hyden, before I pass you through to Mr. Nolen, let me tell you what happened last week. He went by my desk, backed up and came back. He said to me, 'Angela, you are doing a terrific job; I hear great comments from our employees and great comments from our customers about you. I just want you to know that we appreciate it. You are doing an excellent job. Keep it up.'" Let me tell you something, folks, Angela is on a roll. Angela is awesome. Angela is the uncommon denominator. What did it cost that CEO to stop and give her the positive KITA? Obviously nothing. This is what I call, "giving away the sleeves from your vest."

CREATE HEROES AND CHAMPIONS

Reward and recognition can be more powerful than cash and bonuses. Let me give you an example of a reward structure. An employee team came up with this suggestion. Every suggestion for continuous improvement was written up and put in a glass bowl. One employee might have 50 suggestions during the year, while another might have only one. At the end of the year, the company rented The Price Club for an hour before it opened and all employees attended. The five employees who had contributed the highest number of "continuous improvement suggestions" were the champions of the day. It was sort of like a Miss America Pageant, where there is a 5th runner up, a 4th runner up and so on. The 5th most productive employee and their spouse were given a shopping cart and they had 30 seconds to run down the aisles. Anything they could put in their cart in that time, they could keep. The 4th runner up got 60 seconds. Each couple got more time, up to the number one couple, who got two minutes. Then, after all that was completed, with much cheering and yelling, everyone went outside for a recognition barbecue.

Management needs to create heroes and champions in the organization. They need to identify the employees that are embracing customer focus, spotting problems, redesigning the processes, eliminating the defects and errors, and adding value to the customer. Then they need to make them the heroes and champions in the business. But this shouldn't be done on just a one-on-one basis . . . .

Let's assume that an employee came up with a great idea. Should I, as that employee's manager, single him or her out, in a one-on-one situation, and say, "Sven (or Lena), that was really an awesome idea. I really appreciate it." Or would I be better off giving that employee their positive KITA in front of their peers? I'm going to suggest that if you want to change the organization, if you want to embrace customer focus, and if you want to get more ideas out of your employees, you need to create heroes and champions, AND the best way to do that is to reward awesome behavior publicly in front of their peers.

The bottom line:
reward publically;
criticize privately.

TURNOVER IS VERY EXPENSIVE

When a company invests in their employees in terms of training and rewards, and they give employees recognition for great performance, it creates an exciting company environment that can contribute to reducing employee turnover. High employee turnover usually results in lower customer satisfaction, which can result in higher customer turnover. High employee turnover can also result in much higher costs for the company. Turnover is expensive. The cost of turnover has been calculated as seven times the annual salary of the employee. Although this number may be slightly lower for some types of employees, often it is even higher. Does your company have an account number labeled "The Cost of Turnover"? This can be a huge expense; however, we don't see it when we are in those financial meetings dissecting P&L (the Profit & Loss Statement).

| Account #XXXXX | NOT COMMUNICATING | $$$ Millions |

TRUE Cost of TURNOVER

ANNUAL SALARY

Sales Rep	$ _____
Technician	$ _____
Bookkeeper	$ _____
Sub Total	$ _____ x 7 = $ _____

To calculate the cost of turnover, list all positions where you lost an employee, i.e., those employees that you didn't want to lose, not those that were "weeded." Next, annualize their salary. If they started in February and left in November, total their salary for those months, and then divide by the number of months to give you their average monthly salary. Then multiply this number by twelve to get their annualized salary.

The cost of turnover is seven times the employee's annual salary. So multiply the sum total of the annual salaries by seven and you get the true cost of turnover. Turnover is not just the cost of running an ad in the newspaper and the time required for interviewing, etc. The cost of turnover includes the learning curve of new employees as they get up to speed and get to a point where they are as valuable to the organization as the employees that left. It also includes the amount of time spent by others training and assisting the new hire, an activity that detracts from their productivity in their respective jobs.

REWARDING THE RIGHT STUFF VS. THE WRONG STUFF

Now, let's take a look at some examples of rewarding the right stuff vs. rewarding the wrong stuff. In many cases, what I experience while looking at client organizations is a lack of congruence between what the company is trying

64

to do and what's getting rewarded. Be careful when putting in an incentive program to encourage "the right stuff"; it could backfire.

In another case, a manufacturer was shipping products out to their customers, and 20% of the products they shipped came back with quality problems—20%! The cost of that was enormous! What I found out was that the employees on the factory floor were being paid by the "number of piece parts." They were paid based on how many they could crank out per hour. I'm not against productivity measurement systems or incentives for productivity. However, in this case, perhaps they needed to add some quality goals as part of the employees' pay system.

Don't Back Off in Tough Times; Counterintuitive Thinking May be the Right Strategy

Sales Representatives: It is critical to take care of your top reps during difficult times. Compensation and incentives can play a huge role in increasing sales. If your competitors are in the process of merging, this may be a great time to hire their best reps or other staff. Instead of cutting incentives, contests and trips, it might be timely to increase your efforts in these areas.

Leadership: In tough times, managers need to start exhibiting inspired leadership traits! Communication is critical. Don't let the employees get their information from the rumor mill. In a down economy, if you tell your employees "we're going to have a tough year," they just might prove you right.

Training: Most companies pull back on training in tough times, but they should do the opposite. If they invest in their employees, it will increase their competitive advantage. I had a CEO call me and say, "We need to lay off 15% of our employees because our industry is going through tough times. I want your team scheduled on the calendar before we announce the layoffs. I want the 'survivors' to get trained on adding value for the customer, so we can have a good year." What kind of year do you think he had?

No Whining and Complaining: In tough times, some people tend to whine and complain. Their mantra is . . . "This used to be a fun industry." There should be a $10 fine for whining. Let your competitors do all the whining. In tough times, the winners will be the ones that find opportunities; encourage your employees to come up with great ideas.

Counterintuitive Thinking: Life is a six-inch game, and that six inches is right between the ears. If you tell your employees that the economy is tough and we're going to have a tough year, they just might prove you right. Instead, tell your employees that even though the economy is tough and our competitors think they will have a tough year, let's put the pedal to the metal and bring more value to our customers and have a good year. They just might prove you right. I would never lie to employees; however, telling them we're going to have a tough year is probably not the best strategy.

STEP 6: HAVE FUN!

Now let's go to the last step in making your employees the weapon. This step is simple – make it fun! Employees want to have fun. They don't want to be bored; they don't want to be in a negative or backstabbing environment; they don't want to get beat up. They want to enjoy what they are doing. I'm going to suggest that if they enjoy what they are doing, you are going to get much better results: much better productivity, much better quality, much better results in terms of zero defects. And it's much more fun and exciting for them to be working for a high quality, winning company. So, get off any negative stuff and get with the positive stuff.

Celebrate the little successes. Celebrate the little things on a regular basis. Don't wait. And when you do celebrate, make it fun.

Do some outrageous things too. I can still picture Sam Walton, who told his employees, "If you hit this kind of profit, I'll do the hula on Wall Street." They did, and he did. How many employees do you think really just wanted to see him do that? Seems a little outrageous, but think about the fun and the excitement generated in the organization.

Southwest Airlines is an example of where the employees have fun doing their jobs. On a flight not too long ago, our departure was delayed. Rather than have the passengers get antsy because of the delayed takeoff, the flight attendants engaged the passengers in a fun quiz. Several flight attendants stood in the aisle holding up rolls of toilet paper. One flight attendant announced that they were going to have a contest to see which passenger could figure out how many individual sheets of toilet paper it would take to go all the way from the cockpit door to the rear of the airplane. The passenger that came closest to the exact count would win a bottle of wine.

The flight attendants proceeded to unroll the toilet paper and stretched it from the front of the plane all the way to the rear. Now being an engineer and slightly competitive, I thought, "I've got to win this contest!" I counted the exact number of tissues from the seat in front of me to immediately behind me. Therefore I knew exactly how many sheets it would take per row. Then I proceeded to count the number of flight attendant call buttons from the front of the plane to the rear of the plane. I multiplied that number times the number of sheets per row. Then I added a few extra sheets for the exit row as well as the number of sheets I thought it would take for the restroom area. We each had to write down our seat number and our guess and share it with the persons sitting in the same row so they could verify our numbers.

I was feeling fairly confident when I saw the estimates by the people sitting adjacent to me, as they were significantly different than my own. When the flight attendants stated, "Raise your hand if you have more than 200," several hands went up. Then they said, "If over 250, keep your hand up." As they zeroed in on the actual count, there were only two hands up—mine and a lady two rows in front of me. When they announced the actual number, I had missed by only one sheet. The lady had nailed it exactly. When they asked her how she figured it out, she said, "I just guessed." I think I should give that lady some money and have her buy a lotto ticket for me.

When the flight was delayed, the employees at Southwest could have let the passengers sit there and get antsy or frustrated. Instead, they diverted their attention and created a fun interlude.

Tip: In your organization, if something is delayed or late and your customers are sitting or standing idle, what fun activity can you engage your customers in to take their mind off the delay?

Your employees are either your competitive advantage or your competitive disadvantage. It's your choice! So what are they in your organization?

GROWING VALUE FOR YOUR INTERNAL CUSTOMERS

ADDING VALUE TO YOUR INTERNAL CUSTOMERS IS THE FIRST STEP TOWARD ADDING VALUE TO YOUR EXTERNAL CUSTOMERS.

*The grass is not greener on the other side of the hill;
It's greener where you water it.*
- Howard

If you want to add value to your *external customers*, there is a critical strategy—and it's one that revolves around your employees. Once your employees understand that they are the uncommon denominator, and that they are the competitive advantage for your organization, they will understand the importance of adding value to the customer. Then, it will also be easy for them to see the advantage of adding value to their relationships *within* the organization. In other words, they need to add value to their *internal customers*.

We know what we are, but not what we may be. - William Shakespeare

Too frequently, employees look at their relationship with an internal customer as more of an attitude. Let's work together and be friendly to each other, etc. This is good, but they also have to figure out how to add value to their internal customers.

Start with the fundamental definition of the internal customer. The internal customer is the person that receives the output of your work. If an employee

69

creates a form and gives it to another employee, the employee that receives the form is the internal customer. The provider of the form is the internal supplier. We are going to marry the concept of the "internal customer" with the concept of "outside-in." We're going to uncover serious opportunities and increase the value to internal customers. This will result in increasing value to your external customers.

PERSONAL EXAMPLE: SENIOR MANAGEMENT AND ACCOUNTING

When I was a senior executive for a Fortune 100 Company, I designed a tool to help internal customers and internal suppliers figure out how the internal supplier could bring more value by becoming more "outside-in." A separate form was used for each internal supplier/internal customer relationship. As an example, let's use the accounting department, with senior management as their customer. On the internal supplier form, the supplier lists the various products or deliverables that they produce. It is key to talk about specific deliverables as opposed to talking in generalities.

The accounting department listed as their product/deliverables: the P&L (income statement), balance sheet, sales report, accounts receivable report, etc. Then the senior executives rated their accounting department (internal supplier) on whether or not these deliverables were "inside-out" or "outside-in". One of these deliverables was a Sales Report, which listed all of the sales reps, what their quota was, what they sold for the month, and what their percent of quota was. However, the report was alphabetical by sales rep. So when the senior executives got the report, we would have to scan through the pages to try to figure out which sales rep had the highest percentage, and who was number two and number three, etc. It was not easy for us to quickly determine which of our sales reps were well ahead of quota and which were behind.

This was the reason that this particular product/deliverable was rated "inside-out." During the discussion on how to convert the sales report to an "O" (outside-in), I said, "It would be great if you could print the report by ranking the sales reps by percent of quota for the month. This way we could easily look at the report and know instantly which of our reps were ahead of or behind quota." Then I asked if we could get the same format for year-to-date. Obviously, making the report more "outside-in" created much more value for the senior management team.

Case Study: Perry's Ice Cream was probably not unlike many other small manufacturing companies. They had a niche and were good at making their product.

The employees at Perry's ice cream went through an exercise to determine who their internal customers were. Where were they adding value for their internal customers? Were they doing it their way or the internal customer's way?

When employees were brainstorming on the internal customer concept, they shared the following experience. Each department had its own unique processes with its own set of priorities. Palletizing, for example, was responsible for sorting and stacking ice cream as it came to them from production and then delivering it in palletized units to the frozen warehouse. The frozen warehouse was responsible for receiving and storing the product as well as acting as a fully functional distribution center. The processes in the warehouse were a combination of shipping and receiving, designed to support the order fulfillment of daily direct store routing. This was a labor intensive process that required access to all of the stock-keeping units (SKUs) in the warehouse within a specific time window.

As with many warehousing operations, space is the commodity around which all processes flow. Every move in and out must be timed in a precise choreography of space management, where small defects can have devastating effects to productivity, as it often did at Perry's Ice Cream. Into this environment, palletizing would send a steady flow of inventory and create what the frozen warehouse workers called "gridlock." Communication between the departments was virtually nonexistent and the governing philosophy could be characterized as "just deal with it."

The drivers used 18-wheelers to deliver ice cream to customers such as supermarkets, and the driver would pull up to get a new load at the frozen warehouse. Drivers waiting for loads were frequently asked to "go grab lunch" to allow the warehouse time to move product from one aisle to the next in a frustrating process of double handling. The reason the frozen warehouse employees had to move that ice cream out of the way is that the employees that moved the ice cream from the manufacturing floor to the frozen warehouse placed the ice cream where it was convenient for them, *not* where it was convenient for the warehouse employees.

I often refer to this as having an MIT degree, which stands for "Move It Twice." Occasionally, some company employees move it thrice, which probably means they have their PhD in this inefficiency. This represents a significant amount of non-value added time, and it's unlikely you could charge the customer for all this incremental labor.

Once the driver arrived at the supermarket, the driver used a hand truck or dolly to move the ice cream from the parking lot to the refrigerated cases inside the super market. The dolly was bought by the Purchasing department. Purchasing, however, had never really solicited the drivers for input in terms of what type of dolly would be best suited for their purposes. These dollies were stored in the yard alongside the truck in the mud and snow. The configuration of the dolly was such that occasionally the dollies' lower plates would hit the cases of ice cream.

Step 1: During the brainstorming on the internal customer exercise, the employees were asked to identify which departments were the internal customers and which were the internal suppliers, and how the suppliers were adding value to their internal customers. Here are their results:

The frozen warehouse was a supplier to the drivers. The forklift operators were suppliers to the frozen warehouse, and Purchasing was a supplier to the drivers.

Step 2: The next step in the exercise was for the internal customers to evaluate their internal suppliers by looking at several dimensions through the eyes of the customer. One dimension evaluated whether or not the internal suppliers' perspectives could be characterized as "inside-out (In-Out)" or "outside-in (Out-In)." Another dimension evaluated the internal suppliers in terms of their level of quality and service.

The quality of service might be things like how timely the internal supplier was. Was the internal supplier operating on their timeline or that of their internal customers?

The perception of a minute depends on which side of the bathroom door you are on. — Howard

It's not the internal suppliers' watch that matters; it's their customers'!

The quality of service might be things like how complete the paperwork was, as well as how accurate. Every definition of quality, from Dr. W. Edwards Deming to any other quality guru, defines quality from the customer's perspective.

The ratings were very telling:

Perry's Ice Cream employees were all very excited. Having their internal suppliers become "outside-in" gratified the internal customers. The suppliers were equally as excited because they were all, finally, working together as a team.

As many times as this exercise has been done, with companies looking at 15 or more relationships, well over 90% of the ratings have been similar, that is, the internal suppliers have been rated as "inside-out" and their quality and service was rated low.

Note: This exercise is not about putting down other employees; it is all about finding opportunities to increase value. The assumption of this exercise is that if the internal suppliers bring more value to their internal customers, then obviously the organization can bring more value to their external customers.

When Old Habits Pop Up . . .

Rick Jory of Sandhill Scientific hired me to do a speech on Customer Focus to his team. To say that Rick was passionate about this subject was an understatement. His company engaged a marketing communications firm to design a new logo for the company and then they had caps made for the event. These were unusual caps. They had two brims. On the front was their new logo with the words "Outside-In" and on the back was their old logo with the words "Inside-Out." After my presentation he said, "This is the beginning of a new era for our organization. We not only have a new logo and marketing materials; we have a new way of thinking. The old logo represented our prior way of thinking: 'inside-out.' Our new logo represents our way of thinking going forward, which is 'outside-in.'"

He then announced that, during the rest of the meeting, if anyone witnessed "inside-out" thinking they were to take their cap and switch the bill so that the old logo faced forward, i.e. the company had returned to "old habits" and whatever had just been said represented "inside-out" thinking.

Within 30 minutes of my presentation, Rick and his team were demonstrating a new piece of medical equipment. A nurse in the audience complained of a feature that was missing on the new product – a product used by nurses. Rick immediately defended his engineering team and began to list reasons why that feature had been left out. Whoops! During this defense, everyone picked up their hat and switched the bill to "inside-out." After turning beet red, Rick seized the moment to make a critical point. He said, "Okay. That demonstrates just how easy it is to fall prey to looking at things through our own eyes, instead of the customer's. It's clear that we all have to shift our thinking, and that definitely includes me."

I felt that Rick clearly modeled the behavior that he was expecting from his team. He did not fall trap to the "do as I say, not as I do" mindset. He was willing to use himself as an example and that made a powerful statement. Rick's behavior was a great example of what management needs to do. Unfortunately, it doesn't happen nearly enough in most companies.

TEAM EXCELLENCE

A long, long time ago, when I was a corporate executive, I called the departments together to talk about teamwork. Teamwork is certainly not anything new. Coach K. from Duke, Vince Lombardi, John Wooden and countless executive consultants have all done their spiel on teamwork. Who can argue the hazards of not functioning as a team? My observation was that each department was focusing on doing an awesome job at whatever that department's role was. For example, sales employees were focusing on being awesome at selling, and the executive in charge of sales had her attention focused on her role in meeting the goals of her department. The same held true for operations and all other departments.

FUNCTIONAL EXCELLENCE

I called a meeting and drew a chart. I said, "Each department is focusing on being five-star in their particular area. Five-star in terms of sales, accounting, operations, etc."

I then said, "Although being excellent in whatever functional department you work in is good, it is also important to strive to be five-star at team excellence. In other words, it's nice if you are an All-Star shortstop and another person is an

TEAM EXCELLENCE

All-Star second baseman; however, if you cannot turn a double play together, what good is it? Being five-star together is far more important than being five-star individually. As an overall philosophy, team excellence will win over individual excellence every time.

A classic example of what I'm talking about is the 1980 US hockey team. Herb Brooks was the coach. When he was putting his team together, he did not select a couple of players that were favored superstars. He got incredible pressure from the board of directors and others to do just that. However, Herb had designed a strategy to beat the Russian team. He wanted players that could work together as a team. I can't think of a better example of team excellence than the 1980 US hockey team that defeated the heavily favored Russians.

Tip: Have a discussion about what team excellence means versus functional excellence: a quick review of "inside-out" and "outside-in," and then introduce the internal customer worksheet. This can be an extremely important exercise that will excite your employees and increase your competitive edge. It may be beneficial to have two or three employees from different departments get together to brainstorm ways that they can be five-star together.

The problem is exacerbated by having a manager in charge of each function. The sales executive is focused on sales, the financial executive is focused on financials, the operations executive is focused on operations; however, no one is focused on managing the relationship between departments. This scenario results in infighting and finger pointing. Departments frequently view their relationship as a win-lose. If sales wins, we lose, or vice versa. No one is managing team excellence. Team excellence, in my opinion, is far more important than functional excellence.

How good are your employees at growing value for their internal customers? Forget about it if they are thinking "inside-out."

Are You Leaving
Money on the Table?

If you want to give it away, my grandmother could be a sales rep.
- Howard

In today's highly competitive environment, the battlefield is strewn with companies whining and complaining about competing on price.

The typical reason companies are trapped into competing on price is that they don't bring any more value to the customer than their competition. Obviously, companies want customers and prospects to select them over the competition. Secondly, they really don't want to drop their price. Too often they think it is unfair or even unrealistic for customers to pressure them to reduce their price.

Customers and prospects are "commoditizing" their suppliers. They treat them as though they are all equal, basically demanding they drop their price if they want to get their business. And suppliers frequently blame the customers or the market environment for this dilemma. But perhaps they are pointing the finger in the wrong direction. . . . Those companies that are complaining about competing on price have spent more time grousing about it than convening meetings to find more ways to add value for the customers. My experience has taught me that far too many companies talk about adding value at their annual offsite strategic planning meeting but rarely thereafter.

MAKE SURE THE CUSTOMER UNDERSTANDS YOUR ADDED VALUE

If an organization gets hammered day in and day out on price, it can take this next statement to the bank: "The customer does not understand your added value." Either you have added value, but you did a lousy job of communicating it, or worse, you don't have any added value.

HERE ARE THREE TIPS TO RAISE YOUR PRICE:

Tip 1: Have a brainstorming session to determine and document your added value.

Tip 2: Brainstorm how your organization could do a much better job of communicating your added value.

Tip 3: Have a brainstorming meeting to discuss various media to communicate your added value.

Companies need to consider multimedia when communicating their added value. Multimedia options to consider include:

- Website
- Newsletters
- Sales rep presentations
- Proposals/Quotes
- Executive visits
- Social media—Web 2.0

Website: Do you have an "awesome" description of your added value on your website? Do you have streaming video of a customer articulating your added value on your website? Do you have testimonials, by market segment, on your website? Does your website have any tools, tips, how-to's, streaming videos or other useful resources?

After speaking at the annual meeting for Petroleum Equipment Institute (PEI), the executive director was very generous in telling my staff that "Howard was the best speaker we've had in 10 years!" My staff must have given him a big tip. They asked him if he wouldn't mind saying that on camera. He sent us streaming video of his comments. Where do you suppose we put that video?

Here is an interesting question: "What percentage of companies have streaming video of customers articulating their added value?" I put this question to people all the time, and the number who actually have it is minimal. Does this represent an enormous upside potential or what? Go to www.howardhyden.com and check out the streaming video.

How about putting tools on your website? Justblinds.com uses video to great effect on their website and we will discuss this and other tools in chapter eight.

Newsletters: Rich Mattern, when he was president of Raymond Handling Solutions, called me and said, "Three customers called his company to say they hadn't received their newsletter and asked if they could get a copy." He explained to me that the customers thought the newsletters came out on the first of the month, when actually they weren't due out until the 15th. Rich assured the customers that their newsletter would be coming shortly. How good does it get when your customers call you wanting your newsletter? Raymond Handling's customers are excited about what Raymond's employees are doing that add value because just maybe the customer can use the same idea in their own company. Now that's adding value. Rich Mattern is another one of our awesome clients who clearly "gets it" and drinks the customer focus Kool-Aid.

Does your organization use newsletters to communicate your added value? What if you included a different story every month, highlighting how one of your employees went the extra mile and added value? Would a series of these newsletters going to customers help customer retention? How about including a copy of these newsletters in the appendix? What could that do to the close rate?

- Increase close rate
- Increase customer retention

Sales Rep Presentations: Do your sales people have an awesome description of your company's "added value" in their sales presentation, whether they do it verbally or as part of their Keynote (PowerPoint for average PC users)? Do the sales people have quantifiable data on that added value? Do the reps have a picture—or better yet, streaming video on an iPad—talking about your added value? If you sell through dealers, independent manufacturing reps, or distributors, have you crafted an awesome presentation for them with the above tips?

Proposals and quotes: Is there an awesome statement about your added value in your proposal and/or quote? Have you quantified your added value in your proposal or quote? Is there a testimonial letter from a customer articulating that added value in your proposal or quote?

My experience has taught me that proposals are often an underutilized opportunity to increase sales. I've even witnessed some awesome companies that have only average proposals. This results in a very frustrating situation where companies know for a fact that they're better than the competition, but when it comes to winning over a new customer, they lose to a competitor. In my opinion, if the company is truly more awesome than the competition, but they lose the sale, this probably means that they teed themselves up in such a way that allowed the competitor to pick them off.

Frequently, companies will allow customers to perceive them as being equal to the competitor. This results in the customer thinking that all competitors are a commodity. The net result is competing on price. The way to battle this is to develop a more awesome proposal than the competition.

Executive Visits: Think about when your executives or managers visit customers. This is another communication touch point with your customers. Do these managers share a story about what one of your employees did for a customer, even if it's not specific to this customer? Or does your management team say, "How are we doing?"

How are we doing? . . . are you kidding me? Is that average or awesome? Our mom taught all of us, "If you can't say anything nice, don't say anything at all." Your customer's mother taught the same lesson. If you ask "How are we doing?" you will probably get the proverbial "Fine." You can't be serious about playing the game at the awesome level with this approach. Tell the customer, "Since 'no one is perfect' is a statement everyone will agree with—except maybe your wife—it gives you permission to talk about our warts. Do you think there are any areas where we might be a C- and need to improve?"

Or try this: "We are committed to continuously raising the bar for our customers, and we'd love to get your help as to where we could raise the bar." How about standing or sitting there with a small spiral notebook or blank tablet and a pen ready to write down what the customer suggests? What does that communicate to the customer versus standing there with a cup of coffee in your hand saying, "How are we doing?"

Your competitors are probably saying, "How are we doing?" Think about it: there is so much mediocrity in today's highly competitive environment. The void of awesome represents a serious opportunity for those willing to step it up.

Another tip is to bring a copy of your newsletter that highlights a story about one of your employees going the extra mile and share it with your customer. Many of our clients have commented that their customers love getting these tips and stories because they can use them in their business. Don't forget to point that out to the customer.

• **Social Media:** Web 2.0 has arrived, and many businesses are using Twitter, Facebook, and LinkedIn to connect to their customers, as well as to potential customers. Many business leaders, including yours truly, thought social media was for those who wanted to share personal and family information and photos. While that is true, many of us did not recognize the marketing potential for our businesses. Social media is another media your organization should consider using to communicate awesome examples of your employees adding value.

After a speaking engagement in Orlando, the VP of marketing for a Florida company wrote an article paraphrasing my presentation. She attributed the content to me and included a picture of me with her article. She then tweeted to over 200 of her clients about the tips on customer focus. She recognized this as an opportunity to add value. When my staff showed it to me, it hit me like a ton of bricks. I am a propeller head, and I thought social media was for teenagers. I missed it completely. We have now hired a social media consultant who is developing a social marketing plan for us. Web 2.0 has grown and will continue to grow even further as a critical marketing tool.

In summary, rate your organization's effectiveness in terms of communicating your added value using multimedia. Then figure out what you have to do to get an A or A+.

MULTI-MEDIA	GRADE	ACTION REQUIRED
1) Website	A B C D E F	○
2) Newsletters	A B C D E F	○
3) Sales Presentations	A B C D E F	○
4) Proposals/Quotes	A B C D E F	○
5) Executive Visits	A B C D E F	○
6) Web 3.0/Social Media	A B C D E F	○
7) All of the Above	A B C D E F	○

At an Association meeting in Dallas, I asked the audience of 250 members to rate their organization's effectiveness in using multiple media to communicate their added value. I asked them to grade themselves from A to F.

I then asked all those that gave their organization an A to raise their hands. No hands went up. When I asked all those that rated their organization a B to raise their hands, two hands went up. I asked all those that rated their organization a C to raise their hands and three or four hands went up.

I didn't want to embarrass anybody, so I asked all those that rated their organization a D, E, or F to raise their hands, and the rest of the audience raised their hands. I then asked for a show of hands on all those that felt their organization had serious work to do in terms of communicating their added value. Every hand in the room went up.

It has been my experience that even those companies that I would rate as A or A+ in terms of adding value to customers, I would rate as C– in terms of their effectiveness at communicating their added value using multiple media—and that is being kind.

That right there should be worth hundreds of thousands of dollars, if not millions. Therefore, you could now afford to buy 1,000 copies of this book and mail them to all your customers as a way of bringing value to them!

In normal economic times, and even more so in tough economic times, it is extremely important to bring more value to your customers and prospects relative to your competition. Our clients are typically the A and B players who want to take it to an A+. I would give them a rating of A or A+ at implementing ideas that will add value and I would rate them as C– at communicating their added value.

This is a huge missed opportunity!

Here is an interesting question: Think of your chart of accounts and ask yourself, "Do I have an account number labeled 'The cost of not communicating my added value'?" I have lots of experience as a corporate executive in sitting in P&L meetings beating up the numbers and arguing about travel expenses, office supplies, etc. Management always has time to discuss the piddly stuff, but what about discussing the cost of not communicating the company's added value?

Account #XXXXX	NOT COMMUNICATING	$$$ Millions

KNOW WHAT THE CUSTOMER NEEDS BEFORE YOU CREATE YOUR PROPOSAL

Vistage International is an organization of CEOs. Each Vistage group contains approximately fifteen CEOs and they meet monthly, often inviting an expert resource to make a morning presentation. The chairman of a recent group that I presented to in Irvine, California learned prior to the meeting that one of his members had recently lost a piece of business. The feedback from the customer had been, "They are not as customer focused as they should be and didn't listen to us." The member company had partnered with another company to develop the proposal, and the partner had said, "We have read their Request for Proposal (RFP), and we think it would be better if we propose what we believe would be best, instead of what they have in the RFP."

I thought (but didn't say it): "Arrogance can be expensive." The chairman wanted the CEO to share his experience with the group before my presentation. It was an absolutely huge opportunity. The chairman teed me up perfectly and during my presentation, I focused on many of the tips listed below. The group was unanimous in stating that the company lost the bid, even though their price was much cheaper than the competition, due to a bad proposal. Could they have won if they had utilized the tips below?

SEVEN TIPS FOR AWESOME PROPOSALS

TIP ONE: PACKAGING/PRESENTATION QUALITY
Look at the physical appearance of your proposal. Remember, this could be sitting on a desk right next to a competitor's proposal. Now, let me ask you, "What is yours printed on?" Be honest; is it your letterhead? What is the competitor's proposal printed on? Their letterhead! Is your letterhead sexier than the competitor's letterhead? I doubt it.

Think about the presentation of food in a fine restaurant. With a great presentation, you know the food is going to taste great before you even take a bite. It's the same thing with the presentation quality of your proposal. If you're better than the competition, your proposal needs to look better than the competition. WYSIWYG (what you see is what you get) is certainly apropos here.

If your company serves diverse market segments—as an example, schools and casinos—it may be prudent to hire a graphic designer to create unique proposal covers and templates. A photograph of a school that can be ghosted back or some graphic relating to education may be appropriate for the school market. Likewise, a photo of a casino or gambling may be appropriate for the proposal cover for casinos. Using graphics for a proposal template makes a subtle statement to the customer that you specialize in their industry—and it differentiates your proposal from the competitor's.

A company that markets to police departments and fire departments has crafted two different proposal covers. The one for fire departments is in red with ghosted back images of fire trucks, and the one for police is blue with ghosted back images of police cruisers. The message is: "We understand your unique needs." If you want to win in today's marketplace, the days of the generic template are over. Too frequently, companies use a generic template and cut-and-paste something from their last proposal. Does the term "average" come to mind? If you want to play the game at the awesome level, then your proposal needs to be awesome.

TIP TWO: AWESOME DESCRIPTION

You must have an awesome description of your added value. On many occasions I have asked companies if they are better than the competition. Their answer is typically "yes." When I say, "Let's pretend I'm a prospect and you're trying to get me to buy your product or service. Why are you better?" Usually there's 15 minutes of floundering around while they try to explain to me why they are better. When I tell them I haven't heard a significant reason, they continue and usually come up with things that really do matter to a potential customer.

Once they convince me that they are better than the competition, I ask, "Is that in your proposal?" That's when I get the deer in the headlights stare followed by the answer, "No." This is a true tragedy—when a company is better than the competition but they have written an average proposal. Several engineering firms I have worked with fall into this category.

Engineers don't like to write. I know. I am one. I have also witnessed that many companies have a proposal template. Here's trouble! Cut and paste this text from "the template" into a generic proposal and then whine when you don't get the bid.

Define your added value for diverse market segments. Do not use a generic added value or template for proposals. Your value added for "Market Segment A" may be different from your value added for "Market Segment B." Sticking with our earlier example, if you market to both schools and casinos, then you should discuss your added value for each of those segments in different meetings, and then develop two separate statements defining the added value for each segment and include them in the respective proposals.

TIP THREE: QUANTIFY YOUR ADDED VALUE

Many companies are bombarded with requests from customers to lower their price. "Low bid" seems to be the mantra for many organizations, and in many industries it is the norm. Here's an example: A refractory is a company that sells materials that are the liners for foundry ovens. Historically, pricing is all about price per pound or tonnage. Let's assume that if a foundry uses supplier A, the foundry will have to shut down for four weeks. They need to cool down the ovens, remove the worn-out liners and replace them with new materials. However, if the foundry uses supplier B, the foundry will be down for six to eight weeks. Did anyone hear "competitive advantage"?

Did anyone hear "competitive advantage"? - Howard

I said to Company A, "You need to raise your price." To say they were startled was an understatement. I'm sure they thought, "This guy has no idea what he's talking about." I then said, "How much does the customer save if they buy from you and have less downtime?" The response was, "A lot." I said, "How much is a lot?" They said, "A boatload." I said, "How big is the boat?"

If supplier A is competing on a price per pound, they are missing a huge opportunity, and they are leaving money on the table. Supplier A has not calculated how much money their customer saves by using them. They have been bowing to the simple market pressure of "low bid wins." They have been too internally focused on their numbers and the pressure on sales—the bottom line. No doubt they have had plenty of meetings focusing on their P&L, discussing margins, where can they cut expenses, etc. If you work for a public company, the number of P&L meetings can become nauseous. They spend an inordinate amount of time focusing on their numbers. It's a very self-serving culture. Perhaps they would be better served if they spent more time crunching customers' numbers.

Crunch the numbers: In the above example, they need to spend time crunching the numbers to determine how much money they will save the customer. The CFO, VP of sales, and someone from operations should meet to calculate the amount of money the customer will save if they use their company. It might not be a bad idea to invite a customer to participate in the discussion.

Communicate: Communicate this cost saving to the customer. This number needs to appear in every one of their proposals. Highlighting the cost savings as an "added value" will increase the close rate. Reducing the total cost to the customer can take some of the pressure off reducing the price of your product.

Reducing the total cost to the customer can take some of the pressure off reducing the price of your product. - Howard

In many cases, you should consider raising the price, because it's more about the total value equation than about the price. Or perhaps bidding lower, but then adding a sliding scale of bonus money based on the incremental value your company delivers.

TIP FOUR: CUSTOMERS SAY IT BETTER

Once you have quantified your value added, then get testimonial letters from clients articulating the benefits they received from your added value. Personalize it even more by getting a photo of that customer and including it on the testimonial letter. Then include the letter in the back of your proposal in the appendix. You might even get a one-sentence statement from the customer. Put it at the end of the paragraph that talks about your added value so that it is prominently displayed. The customer is now validating your added value.

This technique is called a "pull quote." The quote remains in its original context as well. You see this technique in magazine articles all the time.

Use a pull quote to attract attention or make a "grabber" statement. - Howard

If possible, make sure the testimonial letter you put in the appendix is from the same industry as the prospect you are selling to. In our company, we have hundreds of testimonials. For example, several years ago, I was the keynote speaker at the Casket and Funeral Supply Association of America. We have a testimonial letter from the executive director; he wrote wonderful words about my presentation. Several months later we got a phone call from the Cremation Society of America. It doesn't take an Einstein to figure out the next step. Whose testimonial letter are we going to include in our press kit? Is it going to be from the Plumbers Association or Electrical Contractors?

Get testimonial letters from the various market segments you serve. Organize them in a spreadsheet by industry. Everyone in your company that generates proposals will then have, at their fingertips, the testimonials for the appropriate markets. This should enhance your close rate, not only because of the great testimonials, but also because prospects like to know that you have experience in their industry.

TIP FIVE: CUSTOMERS LIKE THEIR STUFF

Use the customer's logo on your proposal: Customers like to see their own name and logo. I think it might even be more important than your own logo. Make their logo bigger than yours. It makes a statement that you are customer focused.

Caution: be sure you are aware of any policies companies have regarding the use of their logo; some companies have very strict rules regarding logo usage.

Use the customer's font on your proposal: Research the font the customer uses for their company name. Use your default font for the body of the proposal, but use the customer's font when you use their company name. No one else does that; you will separate yourself from the competition before they even get to open the proposal.

A senior HR executive heard one of my presentations. She thought it would be a good idea to have me attend her company's strategic planning meeting to capitalize on my business and marketing experience. They had already contracted with a facilitator who was going to lead the session. She just wanted me to attend the meeting like the other executives. When she approached the CEO, he said "I don't need to have two consultants in attendance; we can use Howard another time." We had sent the HR executive a one-page letter that she proceeded to give to the CEO.

The CEO was leaving for a flight to Germany and the HR executive gave the letter to him to read on the flight. When he got off the plane in Frankfurt, he called her and said, "Hire him! I want him in the strategic planning meeting."

When the HR executive called me I was obviously surprised that they wanted me to attend since she had already communicated that they would wait for another time. When I asked her "What changed his mind?" she said, "When he read your proposal, he noticed that you had spelled our company name using the same font that we use on our letterhead and business cards. etc." The CEO told her, "Anyone that pays that much attention to detail relative to customers, I want in the meeting."

Our proposal uses a standard default font; however, every time we referenced their company name we put it in the same font that they use.

When you write proposals, perhaps they should be more about the customers than you. They like to see their name and their logo. Making their name and logo more prominent than yours signifies that your organization is more customer focused than organizations whose proposals are highlighting their own name or logo.

What does it cost to use the customer's font or logo? Think about it. Run out to Staples and by one of those "easy" buttons so you can hit it when you write your next proposal.

TIP SIX: ON-TIME DELIVERY

Timing. I remember hearing from the CEO of an engineering firm. One of his VPs was notoriously late in getting proposals to their clients. If you are late getting a proposal to a client, what does the client assume about the delivery of your product or service? There is no excuse for being late with a proposal, quote or bid. In fact, this might be a great key indicator to measure. What percentage of the time do you get the proposal or quote to the customer when you said you would? Never, never, never (that would be Never^3—to the 3rd power) be late with a quote or proposal. If you're late, you've struck out before you even get to the batter's box. If you want to find the problem, look in the mirror.

Never, never, never (that would be Never^3 to the 3rd power) be late with a quote or proposal.
- Howard

88

TIP SEVEN: CREATIVE MEDIA TO DELIVER THE PROPOSAL

Always bring more value to the task than was expected. Think about sending your proposal using media other than paper. This is the digital age. Consider having a "Keynote" presentation with sound on a flash drive that the customer can play using an LCD screen so their entire team can watch it. Instead of a customer testimonial letter, substitute streaming video of a customer stating your value added, how much they saved, etc. You can either preprogram the timing or let the customer advance the slides.

Now, if you really want to step it up and play the game at the awesome level, put your presentation on an iPad. I realize that if you sell a low-ticket item, this may be a tad pricey; however, for less than $1,000, you can make the competition irrelevant . . . well, just about. Using an iPad allows you to have streaming video of your employees discussing your added value, support, etc. In addition, you might want to include streaming video of a customer or two articulating your added value.

Giving the customer an iPad with your proposal on it could be a cool way to separate your organization from the pack. You may want to design your own wallpaper with your company's logo, appropriate text, etc. Obviously, if the price point of your product is too low to justify giving away an iPad then you won't do it; however, the majority of B2B companies are selling larger-ticket items and an iPad can be a great way to show your creativity.

The bottom line is that there are way too many average proposals coming out of awesome companies. Step it up and generate more awesome proposals. This could dramatically increase your close rate. This is critical in normal economic times, and even more critical when times are tough.

SUMMARY OF SEVEN TIPS FOR AWESOME PROPOSALS

1. **Awesome packaging**
2. **Awesome description of added value**
3. **Quantify your added value**
4. **Customers say it better**
5. **Customers like *their* stuff**
6. **On-time delivery**
7. **Creative media**

By not factoring in the tips listed above, is it possible you are leaving money on the table?

AVERAGE REP VS. AWESOME REP

Dropping your price? There's so much discussion on price. Have you ever heard the statement, "I notice you are more expensive than the competition?" Then the rep comes back to management and says, "We have to sharpen our pencil and lower our price or we won't get the business." Are you relating to this? Let's discuss the difference between an average rep and an awesome rep. Which one hates the statement: "I notice you're more expensive than the competition"? The average rep! When they hear that statement they fumble, stutter and stammer. They don't know what to say or do. They go back to their manager and beg them to drop the price.

The awesome rep throws his or her shoulders back, and says, "I'm glad you noticed and let me tell you why." At that moment the awesome rep has an "awesome answer" relative to the added value the company brings to the table and how it impacts the customer. Awesome reps are eager for the customer to tee up that statement. They're hoping that issue comes up because they have an awesome answer to the comment, "I notice you are more expensive."

Sales Rep - Theresa Kallberg

One of our clients invited me to speak at a big sales meeting. Prior to the meeting, I discussed with the president some topics he wanted me to talk about. He said, "I am sick and tired of the sales force coming back and wanting us to drop our price or match the price of the competition. Can you talk about that?" I said, "Absolutely."

I designed my presentation and the night before the event I was having dinner with the president. The subject of price came up again and I said, "If you want to give it away, my grandmother could be a rep." He laughed and asked me, "Are you going to say that tomorrow? I wish you would." I said, "I hadn't planned on it, but okay." What he did not realize was that on my laptop I have my family tree going back 300 years. On that family tree I have a picture of my grandmother taken in 1907. I put her photo in my presentation.

I told the president, "What we could do is sponsor a contest." When I get to this point in the presentation, I'll ask the reps, "How many of you would like an awesome answer to the 'I notice you're more expensive' question?" The majority of hands will go up. I'll say, "I don't have the answer but I know how to get it. Why don't we have a contest to see who has the best answer?"

The president agreed that, at this point, he would jump up out of his seat and say, "That's an awesome idea." The sales reps would be asked to send their answers to the sales manager by Friday. Then the president, sales manager and anyone else they wanted to include would evaluate the responses from the 75 reps and select the two or three that had the best answers. The winners would win a trip somewhere with their spouse.

Obviously, once they had the best two or three answers, they could disseminate these awesome answers to the rest of the sales force. No longer would the sales people balk or be squeamish when faced with the "I notice you're more expensive" statement.

At the actual event, after I got off the stage, I approached the president and I said, "You may want to expand this contest to more than just the sales reps. Why not let everybody in the company participate? First of all, everybody in the company will be thinking about why you're better than the competition, which is great. And second, it could be someone other than a sales rep that comes up with the best answer. After all, it's the employees who are creating the added value, so they may have a great way to describe it. So why not include everybody?" He agreed.

Tip: Sponsor a contest in your company to see who can come up with the best answer to the statement "I notice you're more expensive." Whatever incentive you select, I can guarantee that the ROI will be staggering.

YOUR APPEARANCE CAN AFFECT THE SALE

I want to share another topic relative to sales people that can make a real difference in successful selling. It's WYSIWYG or "What You See is What You Get." Think about this. Can sales be made based on the physical appearance of the sales rep? Can the length of hair, the hairstyle, etc, impact the customer's perception of your service and quality? What you see is what you get. Is it possible to overdress?

Let's say that your market is the education market; you are selling to school districts. Now, these people don't have tons of money and they are very frugal in making decisions. So as a sales rep, you are calling on these school districts and you show up driving a Mercedes. What is the customer's perception? Probably that your price is too high. So it is possible to overdress. You have to consider your market; consider what your customer's perception might be. Look at the business through their eyes and determine how you will best present yourself to avoid leaving money on the table.

MAKE AN IMPRESSION WITH YOUR FACILITY

Another form of WYSIWYG is the company's physical facility. Let's see how this could impact sales. There is a car dealership that sells a ton of new cars. It's not because their advertising is any better or their sales reps have better closing skills. It's because of what they let the customer see. It's because of WYSIWYG. They designed their facility in such a way that when the customer enters to pick up their car from being serviced, they have to walk down a long corridor to get to the other end of the facility. They designed it this way intentionally. They could have put the cashier, where you pay and get your keys, on the end closest to the entrance. But no, they wanted to make the customer walk down a long hallway to get to the cashier.

On the way, the customer walks by a series of windows. Let me describe what the customer sees when they look through the windows. On the other side are the service bays where the mechanics work on the cars. And by the way, the floor gets washed and waxed three times a day, and the mechanics are wearing white smocks (that's right, white smocks). The cars are washed before they are given to the mechanic. When the mechanic finishes working on a car, and it is backed out of the stall, the mechanic must put away every screwdriver, every socket, every wrench, every pair of pliers, before they begin work on the next car. Now, let me ask you a question. What is your perception of the quality of the brake job your car just got? It's awesome, right? The customer makes a quantum leap between what they see and what they believe they got. I could walk into that service bay and watch the mechanic doing a brake job on my car. Did he do an awesome job? I wouldn't know an awesome brake job if I saw it. I'm not technically qualified to judge a mechanic. I am technically qualified to judge what I see. In this case, the physical facility speaks quality; therefore, I believe I received a quality brake job. It helps sales on the front end when the customer's perception of service on the back end is one of high quality.

SAVE THE CUSTOMER TIME, SAVE THE CUSTOMER MONEY

Have a meeting to brainstorm how you can save the customer time. In most instances, saving the customer time results in saving the customer money. Speed wins. If you're slow, you lose; if you're fast, you win. Lead time, response time, turnaround time, and even the time it takes you to return a phone call can be a disadvantage or a competitive advantage.

Remember our story about the refractory and the foundry earlier in this chapter? When you save the company time, you save the company money.

Speed is the currency of future profits . . . . - Howard

Telephone Message Pad:

To: Date:
From: Time:

Message:

Several clients of ours have instituted a "sunset policy." They guarantee that any customer that calls in will get their phone call returned by sunset of the same business day. Even if they don't have an answer, they will call the customer and say, "I don't have an answer, but I didn't want you to think I forgot about you. I will have your answer by noon tomorrow." That's far better than leaving a customer hanging.

It's ironic that something as simple as the speed of returning a phone call can translate into a competitive advantage. It is appalling how pathetic many businesses are at returning phone calls. Some are very good at returning calls and some are not. I don't know what happened to manners in our society, but my mother and grandmother would roll over in their graves if I didn't return phone calls promptly. It's not rocket science; it's just plain courtesy. Not returning phone calls is arrogant and rude!

Tip: Return phone calls promptly.

CONSIDER THE CUSTOMER'S COST FIRST

Companies are too often focused on their bottom line and not on their customers' bottom line. This can be a huge missed opportunity. A greedy approach focused on increasing sales or the bottom line may not have the desired result. My father taught us to focus more on what you can contribute than on what you can take. If you want to increase your bottom line, it might be a better strategy to help the customer increase their bottom line. A key tip on how to accomplish this is to focus on "reducing the total cost to the customer."

Raymond Handling Solutions, a forklift distributor in Los Angeles, who sells to Lowe's, Home Depot, Costco and others, has adopted this strategy. Their customers' forklift operators cause a significant percentage of their maintenance issues when they run their lift into a post or a piece of equipment, causing damage to the lift truck. The normal action taken by the technician is to order a new piece and replace the damaged component. The part's cost is substantial, not to mention the cost of the labor to replace it.

Ron Gonzales, a Raymond technician, is focused on reducing the total cost to the customer. His outlook is, "Let's save the customer some money." Ron, without asking permission from his manager, went to an auto parts store and purchased a hydraulic jack for $200 with his own money. Ron figured he could use this power jack to straighten a bent frame on a customer's piece of equipment. Avoiding the typical solution of replacing the part would save the customer thousands of dollars. Obviously, his dedication to reducing the total cost to the customer would certainly have a huge impact on increasing customer loyalty. Why would any customer think about switching to a new supplier when they have a technician like Ron dedicated to their success and to saving them money?

When Raymond Handling's team learned of Ron's creative solution, they not only reimbursed Ron for his out-of-pocket costs; they also purchased a few more of these tools to distribute to other techs in the field. We all know that positive word-of-mouth (PWOM) is the most effective form of advertising. While there is no guarantee this customer will spread the PWOM, it is very likely. When Ron and other techs at Raymond Handling show this kind of initiative, it is a safe assumption that customers will spread the PWOM. Should the marketing department make a flyer highlighting Ron's accomplishment? Perhaps Raymond Handling could write an article for their newsletter about how Ron Gonzales saved the customer a boatload of money, and include a photo of Ron with the lift. How about adding it to the appendix of every sales proposal? What would that do to the close rate? I am not a fan of power closing techniques. My premise is that if you need power closing techniques to get the sale, you are selling the wrong stuff.

> *If you need power closing techniques to get the sale, you are selling the wrong stuff.* - Howard

Think of the impact on customer retention if this flyer were given to every customer. Ron isn't an isolated case. Many of the employees at Raymond Handling are "adding value" for the customer. Is there any doubt that handing out flyers to existing customers would solidify customer retention? How could a competitor possibly steal a Raymond account? Also, handing these flyers out to prospects just might increase sales. While Raymond Handling's sales have increased in tough economic times, their competitors' sales have gone down substantially.

TWO MARKETING STRATEGIES: LOW COST PRODUCER OR HIGH VALUE ADDED?

There are two basic marketing strategies to choose from—low cost producer or high value added. I have frequently asked management and employees, "Are you the low cost producer or the high value added?" All too often, the answer I get is "Yes." The problem is they haven't made a conscious decision as to whether they want to be the low cost producer or the high value added. At 9:00 a.m., they are the high value added; then at 10:30 a.m., a sales rep says to the boss, "We need to sharpen our pencil to see what we can do to lower our price or we won't get the deal." Have you heard this in your company?

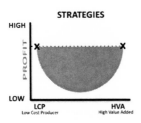

Walmart is the poster child for low cost producer. They have spent decades designing cost out of their operation. They have invested a considerable amount of time as well as money to achieve their low cost position. They have invested in satellite technology to scan their inventory daily and then link their MIS systems to their suppliers, such as Proctor & Gamble, to eliminate redundant functions and drive down costs.

If you are a small business and Walmart comes to town, what is the dumbest thing you can do? That's right … lower your prices. You just walked into the lion's den. Low cost producer (LCP) is a viable marketing strategy and you can make a lot of money with that strategy, as evidenced by Walmart. Walmart does not tailor or customize their products to meet the needs of individual customers. They purchase in huge quantities to get volume pricing; however, the product on the shelf is the same for every customer. Those companies that pursue and are successful at implementing the high value added (HVA) strategy can also make a lot of money.

The problem comes when you haven't chosen a strategy. Think of the company that is trying to swing the pendulum from LCP to HVA within hours on the same day. Perhaps we could label them "Tweeners." They haven't made a conscious decision to select either strategy; they are somewhere in between. Is it any great surprise that their margins have eroded?

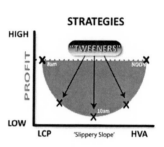

When I spoke at a national association meeting in Cancun, the president of a company approached me after my presentation. He said, "If your chart was a trough and you put a marble at the top of one side and there was a hole in the bottom, my company's marble would roll back and forth and then drop straight out of the bottom." He indicated that his sales reps were letting the customer dictate the price.

VARIABLE PRICING: PRICING ON VALUE, NOT COST

I particularly like to let the price vary, based on the amount of value that the customer receives. The 91 freeway in Southern California is a classic example of variable pricing. This freeway was built with express lanes. Above the fast-track lane they installed electronic displays that would let the drivers know what the rate was if they used the express lane. If the traffic was wide open or moving at a fast pace in the other lanes, the price would be dropped. However, if the other lanes were gridlocked or stopped, then the price of the express lane would go up. In other words, the driver was going to be charged based on how much time they would save using the express lane. This is a classic example of variable pricing. It's up to the customer to choose based on the value they perceive.

FedEx Understands Value to the Customer

When FedEx first started, they charged a flat fee to get the package there by 10:30 a.m. In fact, their slogan was "Absolutely positively by 10:30 a.m." Then they realized that not all customers needed the package there by 10:30, so they started offering afternoon delivery at a lower price. Then they decided they would have a two-day delivery for an even lower price. Now FedEx has introduced a "before 8:00 a.m." service.

Do you think they're going to charge the same price for 8:00 a.m. as they do for 10:30? I don't think so. The point is that FedEx varies the price based on the value to the customer and they let the customer pick the level of service they want.

Can you charge more for a rush job? Obviously the answer is yes. I have observed many companies who are constantly doing rush jobs for customers; however, they charge the same price as for normal delivery times. I always tell them, "You are leaving money on the table." Secondly, if you allow your customer to procrastinate and order at the last minute, and then you don't charge them more for it, who is training who? FedEx has different pricing for different levels of service. Why not apply that same pricing strategy of variable pricing for rush, average, or longer?

Tip: Whenever possible, tie your price to the value that you bring to the customer. That is one sure-fire way to get everyone's eyes focused on looking for more ways to add value.

A Quick Turnaround Time Deserves a Higher Price

What I Wanted . . . When I Wanted

A few years ago, when checking out of my hotel in Las Vegas, I let go of my carry-on bag momentarily so that I could sign the bill. The carry-on bag fell over, as did my computer bag, which was sitting on top of it. Later, when I got on the plane and opened my laptop, my screen was cracked.

Well, I wasn't flying home; I was flying to my next engagement in Milwaukee, Wisconsin. I didn't arrive until 10:30 at night, so there were no computer stores open. I took the yellow pages down to the front desk and asked the young man there to identify the computer dealers that were between the hotel and the airport. I wanted to find one in close proximity where I might be able to get the screen replaced on the way to the airport. He identified three or four computer dealers. In the morning when I called the computer dealers, I had to leave a message because they weren't open yet. I provided the type of Apple laptop and model number and indicated that I needed a new screen. I added that I would call back at break time to see whether or not they could replace the screen.

When I called the first company back, they said, "Drop off the computer; we'll have to send it in and it will take three weeks." I thought this was beyond ridiculous; there was absolutely no way that they were going to get my computer for three weeks. My computer is vital to my business and it would be extraordinarily painful to conduct business without it. When I called the second company to ask if they could service the computer and swap the display on my way to the airport, they responded positively. "We would be happy to do that; we have another one here and it will probably take about 20 minutes." I said, "Done deal."

Let me ask you a question: "Did I ask them what the price would be?" In that situation, it wasn't about whether I could find it for a nickel less at some other place. I needed my computer fixed and I needed it fixed right away. So of course I was willing to pay more compared to the dealer that wanted to send it away for three weeks.

Many employees squirm when I tell them this story. They see themselves in a similar situation. When they call for a service appointment they often hear "Let me check to see when we will be in your zip code area, or neighborhood." Too frequently, companies tell us when they want to deliver the service as opposed to asking us when we need the service. Many service providers are only open during "normal" business hours, yet there are obviously a lot of "abnormal" customers who need service outside typical store hours. And lead time is just one of the many aspects of service that need to be viewed through the customers' eyes. In order to fit specific client needs, companies should offer a wide range of service options including a contingent service policy for rush orders.

Still, many employees feel trapped by a current policy they cannot change. My response is that you MUST CHANGE. The response time for a service request can either be a company's competitive advantage or a competitive disadvantage. It's your pick!

My purpose is to help people get what they want. Once they get what they want, I will get what I want. - Larry Wilson

Is your company competing on "low bid wins"? Do you need to raise your price? The question is, "Are you leaving money on the table?"

PWOM
ESSENTIAL TO YOUR MARKETING STRATEGY

*Get someone else to blow your horn and the sound
will carry twice as far.* - **Will Rogers**

INCREASING VALUE GENERATES PWOM

THE THIRD EGG

The president of a company that I was about to do a workshop for in California wanted me to have breakfast with him the morning of the workshop. We went to a coffee shop and there was a long line. He said, "This place is always packed, and yet there is another coffee shop right down the street that's always half-empty." We waited in line for about 15 minutes and then they took us to our table. As we talked about his company he looked up and said, "That's one of the owners over there, filling up a customer's coffee cup. This place is owned by three Greek brothers and that's one of them." I looked at him and we went back to our conversation.

A few minutes later the owner was at our table filling our coffee cups. I looked at him and said, "I understand you are one of the owners." He nodded. I then said, "This place is packed every day and yet there's a competitor right down the street that is half-empty. What's your secret?" He looked at me and said, "You don't work for them, do you?" I smiled and said, "No, don't worry about it. I live in Colorado." He then said, "It's the third egg." I said, "What does that mean?"

101

He said, "If you go down the street and order breakfast, you get two eggs, hash browns and toast. Here we give the customer the third egg." Then, with a huge grin he said, "Take a guess what the cost of the third egg is . . . a nickel."

The Third Egg is his competitive advantage. Think about it. By giving the Third Egg, he has his customers going all over town spreading the PWOM. He has turned those customers into his best marketing reps. Think about the chart of accounts in his company. Where should he charge the cost of the Third Egg? Cost of goods sold? That would be Average, not Awesome.

If you charge the nickel to a cost account, what perception are you giving to the employees? Is it helping the bottom line or hurting it? Hurting it is the unanimous answer.

How about creating an account number over in the marketing set of numbers under advertising that is not currently used for anything else and labeling it PWOM? Charge the nickel to the PWOM account. That's advertising and it's the best advertising you can possibly get. Now what message are you sending to employees? Is it hurting the bottom line or helping it? Obviously helping it. While you're at it—since it doesn't really affect the bottom line in terms of where you charge it—why not budget money in the PWOM account?

How many companies can you think of that have an account number labeled PWOM? If you said zero, you're wrong. Although the number is small, we have numerous clients who have a PWOM account. They seem to be doing very well. PWOM is a grossly under-utilized marketing strategy!

| Account #XXXXX | PWOM | $$$ Millions |

Tip: Have a meeting with your team to brainstorm the topic "What could our Third Egg be?" I have received many calls over the years with people expressing their excitement about their staff searching for their "Third Egg." Those calls are very rewarding to me.

You will get WOM; the only choice is whether it will be positive or negative! - Howard

PWOM is Less Expensive with Better Results

Everyone knows that positive word-of-mouth is the most effective form of advertising. PWOM is cheaper and gives you referrals, which close at a higher rate. Do you have a PWOM account in your budget?

Whenever there is a major screw-up by your organization, go on the offensive to fix the problem. Make sure to give the customer something "extra." Whatever costs are involved to make the customer happy, the cost of giving something extra to the customer should be charged to this PWOM account. When you select an account number, put it in the marketing or advertising group rather than the cost-of-goods-sold group.

Fixing a serious problem can often convert a hostile customer into your best PWOM sales rep. To play the game at the awesome level, a company should actually budget money in the PWOM account and make sure that employees know what it is and that they are empowered to use it. The money spent on PWOM could also be viewed as an insurance policy against losing the lifetime value of this customer. This should include the cost of the negative word--of-mouth," or NWOM, that this irate customer could spread.

Some of us will do our jobs well, and some of us will not, but we will all be judged by the same thing, the result.
-Vince Lombardi

Now let's analyze the impact that PWOM can have on your P&L.

Consider, company A and company B. For the purposes of this example, let's assume that both companies are equal in revenue and compete in the same marketplace. Company A gets 70% of their business from referrals through PWOM and 30% from paid media. Company B gets 30% of their business from PWOM and 70% of their business from paid media.

COMPANY A		COMPANY B
70%	PWOM	30%
30%	PAID MEDIA	70%

Will the profitability of these two companies be the same? Answer: Not even close. Assume for a moment that I ask a sales rep that question. In one hand, I have 10 leads that came from referrals. In the other, I have 100 leads that came from paid media. You can have one hand or the other; which one do you want? Any rep with a pulse will take the 10 referrals.

There could be 10 times the potential in the 100. Why then should the rep take the lesser number of leads? Because referrals close at a much higher rate than leads generated by paid media. Both organizations are the same size, but company B would need a far larger number of sales reps to obtain the same level of revenue as company A. The organization's sales and marketing productivity would be nowhere near that of company A. Company B would spend more time writing proposals and would need more support staff to help write the proposals. There would be more money spent on marketing, collateral and paid media.

If you have a higher percentage of your business coming from PWOM, is it safe to assume you are bringing more value to the table? If you bring more value you can raise your prices and your margins go up along with the bottom line. You can also make a case that you might lose fewer customers, which also impacts the bottom line.

PWOM can be a huge driver of profitability. However, whenever I ask, "What percentage of your business comes from PWOM?" I get that blank stare. Occasionally, someone will respond, "A lot!" If I ask them, "Is it greater or less than last month or a year ago?" they have no idea. Few companies do an adequate job of developing PWOM as a marketing strategy, let alone measuring it. They do, however, have plenty of time to discuss the many other numbers on the P&L, which are probably insignificant compared to PWOM.

When I was a corporate executive, every business unit that reported to me had money budgeted in a PWOM account. I recall that one year the CFO of the company asked "All your businesses have this PWOM account; what is PWOM?" When I explained PWOM, he said, "That's a no-brainer; we can cut that money out of the budget." I responded by saying, "You can go ahead and cut it out if you want, but I'm instructing my teams to spend the money regardless; you'll just never find it." After a little more spirited conversation, he acquiesced and begrudgingly left the budget alone. I said, "If you're not careful, we'll have to change the meaning of your title, CFO, to mean 'Customer Focus Officer.'"

Tip: The next time your management team is going to have an offsite meeting to develop your company's strategic plan, include PWOM as one of your key strategies. Give your management team a homework assignment to come prepared with ideas regarding what your organization needs to do to generate more PWOM. Secondly, tell them to be prepared to discuss which media will be used to "communicate" your extra value.

In reading the table below, *10 Benefits of PWOM,* note that it may be prudent to keep the number of sales reps high, as well as keeping the marketing/advertising investment high, in order to accelerate your growth. With all the benefits of PWOM, why is it so few companies develop strategies and tactics to create more PWOM, let alone measure the results?

10 BENEFITS OF PWOM

Close Rate	**Referral leads close at a much higher rate than paid media.**
Number of Sales Reps	**The number of reps to get to the same level of sales is less.**
Marketing/Advertising	**It takes less marketing and advertising to get to the same level of revenue.**
Marketing Support	**The amount of staff hours to assist the sales staff in the preparation of proposals and quotes is less.**
Collateral Materials	**Lower costs for marketing literature, collateral materials, etc.**

Higher Margins	If you get a higher percentage of business from PWOM than the competition, you must be bringing more value to the table. This should result in higher margins.
Customer Retention	Higher PWOM is a result of more value. If your organization brings more value, it is safe to say you will have higher customer retention.
Less Employee Turnover	When a company brings more value to the table, reps are happier and the employees who created the value have more pride. Everybody likes to be on a winning team.
Recruiting	When your company is the best-in-class, your organization will become a magnet to attract the best talent in the marketplace.
Costs	When your organization plays the game at the awesome level, you probably have lower costs due to: fewer rejects and returns, lower freight costs, less rework, and less overtime.

"THANK YOU!"

You don't need an MBA or a degree in marketing to figure this one out. My mother and my grandmother ingrained this in my brain when I was little. They constantly said, "Always thank people, particularly if they do something nice for you."

The first time I spoke at the annual Casket & Funeral Supply Association of America, I did not realize until I got to the event that one of the manufacturers, who was a member, contributed all the funds necessary for the association to hire their keynote speaker. I was scheduled to be on first thing in the morning. Meanwhile, I noticed on the schedule that at 11:00 a.m. everyone would be going to the exhibit hall where they could view all the products that were being displayed. The manufacturer who had given the association the money that had allowed them to hire me had a booth in the exhibit hall. I said to the executive director of the association: "Perhaps at the end of my presentation, you or I could announce that Howard will be standing in this manufacturer's booth to answer any questions or just have a dialogue." I felt that this might draw traffic to his booth, which would be a way for me to "add value" for him. Another "Third Egg."

ANOTHER THIRD EGG

Since I preach this stuff, I guess it would make sense for me to follow my own advice. It would be hypocritical if I did not walk the talk.

Upon being booked for PEI's 10-Group General Session at the PEI Annual Convention, I learned that the general attendance had been diminishing over the last few years. PEI 10-Groups are small networking groups of company owners from different regions of North America that have the same size and types of businesses but do not compete with each other. I told Bob Young, an executive with PEI, that I would like to see if we could raise the attendance. I would write an article for their newsletter two months before the meeting to entice the members to attend the meeting. Another Third Egg.

When Bob introduced me, he said, "Look around the room; this place is packed and they're still bringing in chairs. That's a tribute to the speaker you are about to listen to." I was scoring points before I even opened my mouth. I told Bob that, if he was interested, we could invite anyone in the audience who went back and implemented any of the ideas from my presentation to send an email to Bob about what they had implemented and the resulting impact. If Bob would then forward the emails on to me, I would write another article highlighting what had been done. Another Third Egg.

I told Bob that sometimes you can hear a great idea from a speaker but not really "get" the idea until a peer implements it. Then the light comes on. Immediately following my presentation, a chairman of one of the 10-Groups approached me and asked if I would stop by their group's meeting for a few minutes. Another Third Egg. I left their meeting three hours later.

A month later, Bob called my office and hired me to do three presentations at the PEI Service and Construction Managers' Conference in St. Louis that

April. Bob's budget was tight, so he asked if he could have a discount. Since two of the presentations were on the same day and I wouldn't have to fly between speeches, it seemed appropriate to give a discount.

During the conference, I suggested to Bob that, rather than have me just walk into the room where we would have lunch, he could have a VIP table and invite nine people of his choice to sit at my table for lunch, so they could pick my brain, etc. During the session preceding lunch he asked me to stand by the door at the back of the room. After a few announcements, he announced that he was going to read some names and would those people please stand. After he called out all the names, he said, "These individuals will have the honor of having lunch with Howard to pick his brain." The audience gave him an ovation. This wasn't about me; this was about making my client look good, another Third Egg.

ASK FOR PWOM AND SAY "THANK YOU"

As already mentioned, Bob had first hired me in the fall as the keynote speaker for the Petroleum Equipment Institute 10-Group General Session. After the success of that event, I asked Bob, "Since we hit a home run at the fall meeting, would you be willing to generate some PWOM?" His answer was, "Absolutely."

My staff asked Bob if he would forward my press kit to some meeting planners in his network, and Bob's response was awesome. He sent letters to many meeting planners.

PWOM is a seriously underutilized marketing strategy. - Howard

The next time I saw Bob was at the April PEI Conference. During my presentation at that April meeting, I explained the importance of using PWOM as a marketing strategy. I also told the audience to always thank the customer for the PWOM, especially if it turns into business.

At the end of my presentation, I called Bob up to the front of the room and said, "I understand that you sent my press kit to several people in your network."

He nodded affirmatively. I said, "Bob, I just want to thank you," and I reached out to shake his hand. He said, "You're very welcome," and then was about to go back and sit down. I said, "Bob, I'm not through with you yet."

Prior to the April conference, my staff had called Bob's staff to learn what personal activities or sports teams were his favorites. We learned that he had been an avid Philadelphia Phillies' fan since his boyhood days.

As Bob stood there, I said, "I understand you're a Phillies' fan." He grinned, and then I reached in my bag and pulled out a baseball and asked him if he had heard of the person whose autograph was on the baseball. It was autographed by Steve Carlton, a Hall of Fame Philadelphia Phillies' pitcher. Bob was stunned. He had a huge grin on his face, and a huge ovation followed from the audience.

I told Bob the baseball was a token of my appreciation for him spreading the PWOM. The baseball was "outside-in." The fact that my team had taken the time to research our client's interests made the gesture powerful and meaningful for Bob. Another Third Egg.

The baseball cost $115. We could have given Bob a $115 gift certificate for a fine restaurant in his area. Let's analyze the difference between the two choices. First, where is the baseball going to wind up? Exactly! On his desk! Who is he going to think about when he looks at the baseball (besides Steve Carlton)? When people walk in his office and ask him where he got that baseball, who is he going to talk about? Now contrast that with the dinner. Where's the dinner going to wind up? I don't think I need to explain that one; you get the picture. In my opinion, PWOM is a grossly underutilized marketing strategy. The cost of the baseball was charged to our PWOM account.

Tip 1: Ask your best customers to spread the PWOM.

Tip 2: Always thank the customer for the PWOM.

Consider giving a gift, particularly if the PWOM results in a new customer. The only exception to this is when the customer has a policy against receiving gifts from suppliers and vendors. An example would be the federal government, although many politicians seem to be ambivalent about this rule. Also, many large corporations have policies prohibiting their employees from receiving gifts from vendors/suppliers. Obviously, it would not be very customer focused if you did not understand that the customer had such a policy and you put your customer in an awkward position. However, you might be able to ask the customer if there is something else you could do in lieu of a personal gift. Perhaps you could donate to the Susan G. Komen for the Cure, the Boy Scouts, or the Girl Scouts, for example. The client will let you know what would be appropriate.

By the way, do you know of an organization that hires speakers? We would love *your* PWOM. Please call us at 888-559-9711 to refer Howard. If your referral books a speech or workshop, we'll say thank you with a gift.

REPEAT CUSTOMERS ARE LESS EXPENSIVE THAN NEW CUSTOMERS

CUSTOMER RETENTION OFFICER – THE MISSING "C" LEVEL EXECUTIVE

Most organizations have a CEO responsible for the organization, a CFO responsible for the financials, a COO in charge of operations, and a VP responsible for sales. Obviously, each of these executives is responsible for their functional area. So the question is, "Who is responsible for customer retention?" Usually the answer is, "No one." What's missing is a CRO or Customer Retention Officer. Maybe it's time to appoint one.

If you do not want to add a full-time executive to your team, then add the title and responsibility to one of your existing executives. Assign the CRO role to your VP of Sales for six months, then perhaps to the VP of Operations for the next six months, and then perhaps to your CFO. Rotating the responsibility of CRO will give each of your key executives a chance to be engaged in developing and implementing strategies and tactics to increase customer retention. At your monthly executive meetings, have the CRO report on metrics relative to customer retention, in addition to the regular areas. The group should agree on goals for these metrics. Some potential metrics might be: customer retention, percent of on-time delivery, percent right the first time, percent of complete orders, time to fill backorders, number of complaints, response time for complaints, employee retention, employee satisfaction, training investment (dollars invested in training compared to dollars of gross payroll; 5% should be a minimum), and many more.

Who is working harder on your accounts—you or the competitor who's trying to steal them? That might be a scary thought. Developing accountability for customer retention is a great first step on the path to retaining customers.

Who is working harder on your accounts, you or the competitor who's trying to steal them? - Howard

Let's compare two companies:

COMPANY A		COMPANY B
70%	REPEAT CUSTOMERS	30%
30%	NEW CUSTOMERS	70%

Is there going to be a difference in the profitability of the two companies? Obviously, there's going to be a huge difference.

Let's look at the "acquisition cost" of a new account, meaning all the advertising, the proposal preparations, sales rep time, support staff time, marketing literature, etc. The cost of acquiring a new account is huge in comparison to the cost of retaining an existing customer. I have seen data that suggests that it costs five times more to acquire a new customer than it does to keep an existing one. Although that data is several years old, my belief is that the ratio, if anything, has increased. So back to that question again: who is working harder on your existing customers – you to keep them or your competitors to steal them?

Many companies have marketing strategies to get new accounts; however, where is your marketing strategy to keep your current customers? All too often we take our current customers for granted. If you think that customer loyalty is going to happen just because you want your customers to be loyal, you may be in for a rude wakeup call. In addition, schmoozing, golf, and dinner are nice, but they are not profound strategies for retaining customers. Trying to buy loyalty will probably not get the job done.

Here is an example of a problem, but it also presents a great opportunity. We were doing a workshop for a Vistage client who is a fabricator of marble and tile countertops that they sell to contractors. The employees indicated to me that customers "put up" with their company for about a year, then they go to another company and "put up" with this company for about a year, then they go to the third one, the fourth one, the fifth one. "But not to worry, Howard, because, there are only five of us and in about five years we wind up getting them back." Their comment was, "That's just the way it is in our industry."

I asked them what would happen if their company was so awesome that the customers never, ever left to go to another competitor. Playing the hand out for three to five years, what would happen? The employees' comments were, "The competitors would be going out of business." I agreed and also commented it might be possible to acquire one or two of the competitors for a very reasonable price. So understanding that situation, why don't we come up with some strategies that would keep the customers, rather than only focusing on catching new ones and then losing them after a year?

What are the key factors driving customer turnover?

1. NO ADDED VALUE.

In today's highly competitive marketplace, more and more customers are viewing products as a commodity. When customers view products as a commodity, price becomes a serious issue. This has led to such wonders as "Reverse Auction Bidding." To get out of low bid pricing, the answer is "add value" or stay home. If you don't "add more value," you just might "get fired" by your customer.

2. EMPLOYEE TURNOVER BEGETS CUSTOMER TURNOVER.

There is no way that you can have a high level of customer satisfaction if you have a revolving door with your employees. Your turnover should be less than your competitors' turnover. Obviously, some industries may be prone to certain positions having a high turnover, but it's a cop-out just to say "well, in our industry, there's a higher turnover for these people." Your competitors face the same issue; therefore, he who has the lowest turnover wins. Perhaps there needs to be a management meeting to discuss what can be done to lower employee turnover. Customers are sick and tired of training your new hires because of turnover.

Customers are sick and tired of training your new employees because of turnover. - Howard

3. LACK OF ADEQUATE TOOLS TO GET CUSTOMER FEEDBACK.

Too many companies review their internal metrics in meetings; however, they don't have tools to regularly get feedback from customers. Without a serious commitment to learning from customers, it is going to be more difficult to retain them.

Organizations that have a desire to play the game at the awesome level will have a much higher *Learning Velocity* than their competitors. Learning Velocity is a term I coined to connote the speed at which an organization learns from its customers.

You must learn before you earn. - Howard

4. LACK OF EMPLOYEE TRAINING.

When it comes to employee training, you have a choice. A serious commitment to training is a key strategy in companies that excel in customer retention. Companies have made the big investment in terms of the cost of their Human Capital. However, most fall short in terms of their investment in training their employees. "Penny wise, pound foolish" comes to mind. Whether it's Olympians, other top athletes, or musicians playing at Carnegie Hall, we all understand that they didn't get there without a serious commitment to training. Then we drive to work and it's like we had a *You don't know what you* frontal lobotomy—we cut the training budget. *don't know. - Howard* Lack of training also leads to higher employee turnover.

The cost of not training can far exceed the cost of training. - Howard

I have not seen companies that play the game at the awesome level that did not also have a serious commitment to training. The biggest cost is the total cost of your employees. Normally it is the single biggest cost on the P&L and it is a recurring cost. Yet most companies under-invest in their Human Capital. Training should not be looked at as an expense, but rather as an investment in your competitive advantage. A serious commitment to training can increase

113

employee morale, lower turnover, and increase customer satisfaction, all of which result in higher customer retention.

Employees must be viewed as an appreciating asset.
- Howard

5. MANAGEMENT BEHAVIOR.

This is a biggie. Management talks about the P&L, sales, profits, etc. What's missing are questions about customer satisfaction.

When Bill Marriott tours the Marriott properties, 90% of his questions to the field management are questions like: What are you doing to train your employees? What do you hear from guests that they like? What do you hear from guests that they don't like? Only 10% of the questions are about occupancy rates, profits, sales, etc. Do the managers and employees of Marriott think that Bill is serious about guest satisfaction? The answer is obvious because they see it in his behavior.

What type of questions do you typically ask? Employees take their cues from management's behavior. Let's say your company hires a company to conduct a customer survey and schedules a meeting to review the data. Then a scheduling conflict with that meeting occurs with the CEO or other senior executive, and he or she does not attend. This is a signal to all employees that customer satisfaction is not important. My recommendation is that he or she must never let the meeting take place without attending. It would be much simpler to reschedule the survey meeting so you could attend it. By the way, you did have time to attend the meeting on the P&L.

Employees will watch management's behavior, and that behavior speaks louder than anything we say. We may say that retaining customers or customer satisfaction is important, but it really doesn't matter what we say — it matters what we do.

Your videos are louder than your audios. - Howard

Behavior is everything. - Albert Schweitzer

PRICING IS A MARKETING FUNCTION

Pricing is an important topic to discuss in good times. It's even more critical to discuss when times are tough. The financial department within the company often determines the price of the product or service. They analyze the expenses, figure out what margin they want, and then determine the price. In the company I worked for, this was standard procedure. Sure, they got input from the sales reps and a few others. However, pricing was the responsibility of the CFO and his team. I convinced the CEO that we needed to develop our marketing skills so that "marketing became a core competency" for the various business units.

I felt that marketing, as a core competency relative to the competition, would give us a significant competitive advantage. In other words, if the marketing talent in a particular business unit is stronger than that of your competition, you could win. Marketing's role is to analyze the market and determine where to compete (which market segments are attractive and where a competitive advantage can be identified). Marketing also decides where not to compete, through what channels to distribute and sell product, what the product should be and what features it should have, how to promote it, and what the price should be.

Marketing as a core competency can be a significant competitive advantage. - Howard

We typically had a VP of sales and marketing. The second I heard them say "marketing after sales," I knew that they were not really doing marketing. A VP of sales has a marketing person, which is simply sales support. I had to expose them to what real marketing was. I convinced the CEO that we needed to enhance the core competencies of the senior executives in the company. I visited all of the top academic institutions in the country to look at their executive strategic marketing curriculum. I selected 20 of these academic institutions that we could send our executives to—Stanford, Duke, Harvard, Columbia, etc. Typically the programs would only allow two or three executives from the same company, and therefore we needed to make use of multiple programs.

When these executives went to the strategic marketing programs, they came back with their eyes wide open, having discovered that there was a lot more to marketing than just selling. We should never use "marketing" and "selling" interchangeably.

BASE YOUR PRICE ON VALUE

In addition, I went to each business unit and explained to them that "pricing was not an accounting function, but rather a marketing function." That was a shocker for most of the divisions. Then I explained that we were going to determine the price of the product based on the value that we brought to the customer, not on our costs.

Picture a conference room of executives split into two groups. The left side of the table represents company A; the right side of the table represents company B. Company B bases their price on their costs. Company A bases their price on the value that they bring to their customer. Then I simply turn and ask them, "Who is making more money?" The unanimous response is always company A.

COMPANY A	COMPANY B
Price based on VALUE	Price based on COSTS

One of my preliminary assumptions is that if you base your price on the value that you bring to your customer, you will immediately start having more meetings on what you can do to increase the value for your customer. Company "B" will have more meetings on what they can do to squeeze costs out of the equation and increase margins. Don't get me wrong, eliminating waste and ensuring lean manufacturing are good things; however, basing your price on value to the customer just might bring better margins.

Business-to-Business Companies Need to Step Up Their Marketing

Companies have typically been much better at marketing to consumers than marketing business-to-business. Procter & Gamble, Anheuser-Busch, and Coca-Cola are all examples of great marketing to consumers (B2C). If they were poor at marketing, they would get clobbered in the marketplace.

Business-to-business (B2B) companies, on the other hand, have historically been better at sales than at marketing. IBM had a sales culture for decades and there are many other examples of great sales organizations.

B2C companies might get an A or A+ at marketing, but most B2B companies would get a C– (and this might be kind). If you want proof of this, ask any advertising agency what they think of their B2B clients' marketing savvy. Watch their eyes roll.

Rate Your Marketing Competence:

A   B   C   D   E   F

If you rate yourself low, look at it as a great opportunity. If you, as a B2B company, can enhance your marketing skills, you'll have a distinct advantage over your competition. Increase your marketing prowess by hiring a strong marketing person. If you can't afford a full time marketing executive, hire half a one rather than having a full time administrative person. Or hire a marketing consultant. However you can manage it, step up your marketing game.

What is your organization's WOM ratio? Do you have more negative WOM (even though it isn't always expressed) or more positive WOM? Does your organization need to ramp up its marketing core competency?

Counterintuitive Thinking

It's really simple . . . when you get it.
- Howard

Second Derivative Marketing: Focus on Your Customers' Sales Instead of Yours

For those not familiar with calculus, let me give you a quick definition of second derivative using an automobile as an example. First derivative would be the velocity of the car. Velocity = the rate of change in distance over time. The number of miles traveled divided by the time elapsed = velocity. Second derivative would be the "rate of change" in your speed, which is called acceleration. In other words, how fast is your car changing its velocity? Therefore if you want to accelerate your business and speed past the competition, second derivative marketing just might be the right strategy. Focusing on increasing your customers' sales and revenue could result in increasing yours.

When I talk about second derivative marketing, I'm talking about focusing your marketing one step further out in the food chain. I have encouraged a multitude of companies to focus more on their customers' success. What can you do to increase your customers' sales?

First derivative marketing: Companies that focus on increasing their sales. They are working on increasing their *sales velocity*, trying to "speed up their sales."

Second derivative marketing: These companies are focused on helping their *customers* increase their *sales velocity*, which will accelerate their own sales.

First derivative companies focus on their own sales. The impact is on a single company. Companies that actively engage in second derivative marketing are constantly working on designing marketing programs to help their customers increase their sales. Think of the multiplied effect when all your customers increase their sales. When you work on increasing your customers' sales as opposed to your own, it can have a much greater impact on your sales.

A few years ago, I was invited to be the keynote speaker at the Anheuser-Busch annual beer wholesalers' convention. Beer wholesalers from all over the world were coming to Atlanta and I was asked to give a presentation on customer focus. When doing my homework for this presentation, I learned that Anheuser-Busch's market share was staggering. In my opinion, Anheuser-Busch is one of the best marketing companies in the world, not just in the adult beverage market, but in any market. Who is it that wins the top spot for the best commercial during the Super Bowl every year? Anheuser-Busch. Clearly, they are at the top.

Anheuser-Busch divides their customers into two market segments: on-premise, and off-premise. On-premise might be a restaurant or sports stadium. Off-premise would be a liquor store. What is the marketing competency of the person running the local liquor store? I'll bet it's pretty low. Here's one of the best marketing companies in the world selling to a customer that's extremely weak at marketing.

I started my presentation with the Anheuser-Busch logo as my opening slide. I began, "I was thinking about what I would do if I were in your shoes. You're one of the best marketing companies in the world selling to someone who doesn't have any idea how to market." Then I said, "I would stop selling beer."

I paused, and then I repeated, "I would stop selling beer!" The next slide was a photo of a stop sign.

At that moment a senior executive, who was sitting in the front row, turned to the person sitting next to him and whispered in his ear. I couldn't hear what he said, but I think it was probably, "Who hired this guy?" I then said, "I would help the customer sell more beer. Because, if you help the customer sell more beer, then you will sell more beer." Anheuser-Busch does an awesome job of designing marketing programs that help their customers sell more beer.

SPONSORED CUSTOMER SESSIONS

EXAMPLE ONE:

Builders Appliance Center (BAC), a Denver-based company, sells appliances to builders. Last year was an extremely tough year for builders, yet BAC had a good year. Ken Jensen, president of BAC, called and asked me to do a session for his customers and guests, many of whom were builders BAC had never done business with—a "Third Egg" to help them sell more. When Ken opened the half-day session on customer focus, he stated, "We had a good year last year, and we wanted to share some of our success with you. Today, you will get tools and techniques that will help you grow your business." Ken's strategy is to help his customers increase their sales. There were close to 200 customers and guests in that session. It's not difficult to understand why BAC is doing better than the competition. Ken gets it!

When I walked into their lobby, there was a huge sign with a picture of me; it had been in the lobby for the last 30 days and the employees had pointed it out to everyone who walked in, suggesting that they reserve that day on their calendar. How many new customers do you think they got by doing this?

During my presentation, I looked at someone in the audience and asked him, "What percentage of your business comes from PWOM?" I got a confused look. I asked another builder the same question and I got another blank stare. Then I looked at Ken and said, "What percentage of BAC's business comes from PWOM?" He responded, "87.6%."

I looked at one of his customers and said, "What does BAC do in order to get such a high percentage of business coming from referrals?" The builder's response was, "They are awesome and they add a lot of value." I looked at Ken and asked, "Are you satisfied with 87.6%?" He responded, "No, our goal for this year is 95%!" The audience was stunned. Here is a company that gets 87% of their business from referrals and he's not satisfied; now he's targeting 95%. I looked at another builder in the audience and asked him, "What do you suppose they will do in order to increase to 95 %?" He answered, "I'm guessing they are going to add more value and raise the bar even higher." I smiled and said, "Not a bad strategy. You can make that your final answer."

EXAMPLE TWO:

Actually, we have had numerous companies sponsor a Customer Appreciation Session for their clients/ customers. Jim Nordquist is the President of Applied Geotechnical Engineering Consultants, P.C. (AGEC). He felt it would be extremely valuable for his clients to be exposed to many of the tools discussed in our customer-focused workshops. He scheduled a half-day session and invited his clients' prospects, city inspectors, and other contacts. I asked Jim to tell me some of the suggestions they had implemented from our previous workshop so I could incorporate them into my presentation. He really wasn't keen on the idea since he's a very modest guy and didn't want to actively promote his firm. He said, "I want this to be about them and not about us."

I did manage to slip in a couple of AGEC examples without making it a big marketing push for his company. During the mid-morning break, several of his clients told members of the AGEC management team that they didn't realize AGEC offered some other services.

After the session, he treated everyone to lunch. At each roundtable, there was an AGEC manager or employee and several awesome ideas surfaced. The feedback at lunch was extremely positive. So much so, that Jim decided to schedule another event in St. George, Utah.

This event was the "Third Egg" for AGEC. These folks "get it!" They do things right, such as sponsoring this type of an event. Others may say, "If we do an event like this, shouldn't we charge them for it?" Obviously, those folks "don't get it." When you dare to play the game at the awesome level, it sure can be fun. This event was great fun.

EXAMPLE THREE:

Mark Faster, President of Progress Supply, also decided to sponsor a session for his customers. Progress Supply is a wholesaler of heating and air-conditioning equipment and parts. Mark kicked off his customer session with the comment,

"The main purpose of today is to suggest some tools you can use to help you dramatically increase *your* business. However, if Howard says something that you think Progress Supply should be doing, here's what I'd like you to do: we will be hosting a lunch, and we will have a Progress Supply employee at each table so you can discuss any idea that you may have to help us bring more value to you and your business."

The lunch was a huge success and some of the sales reps and managers were bordering on giddy—one-upping each other in terms of what a great idea their table had come up with. It was a great way to get customer feedback. Mark is clearly one who "dares to be awesome!"

Example Four:

Tomar Electronics, another awesome client of the Center for Customer Focus, had a slightly different twist on sponsoring a session for customers. Scott Sikora is president of the company, which was founded by his father. He also has two sisters on his executive team.

After one of the customer focus workshops, the three of them decided that it would be a great idea if they sponsored a session for one of their customers. Blue Max in British Columbia, Canada, is a top distributor for Tomar in the emergency vehicle lighting market. They had just attained a sales milestone, so they were chosen for this gift.

The Tomar senior executive team felt that if they paid for an entire workshop for this distributor, they would come up with tons of suggestions that would help them grow their company—similar to what had happened at Tomar after their other workshop. The strategy was to help their customer grow and as a result Tomar would grow. This type of out-of-the-box thinking is a classic example of second derivative marketing.

Creatively Partner with Your Customers

2J Supply is a wholesale/distributor of HVAC equipment and supplies, and Larry Trimbaugh is one of the owners. He designs programs to help their customers grow their own businesses. Larry calls it their "Partners in Profitability Program." A lot of companies espouse "partnering," but it's mostly rhetoric. This company, on the other hand, is a true partner with their customers; they are seriously focused on helping their customers increase their sales and profit.

2J Supply brings many resources to their customers. One example is advertising. 2J has an advertising agency that develops marketing materials for 2J Supply, and Larry asked the agency to develop marketing materials for 2J's customers as well. 2J doesn't pay for their customers' marketing materials. However, the ad agency has substantial pre-knowledge about 2J's customers, which is a value added for those customers. Since the agency benefits from the economy of scale, 2J's customers realize a cost savings, and, of course, it helps 2J when they help their customers grow their sales.

2J has also worked with their bank and other suppliers in a similar vein, and 2J's customers can likewise affordably avail themselves of these services.

WORKING WITH SUPPLIERS

In addition to working well with your customers, it is important to work well with your suppliers. There needs to be good communication and feedback between businesses and suppliers, and a good partnership means active involvement by both parties. Too often businesses are complacent, expecting the supplier to perform as if on autopilot, without any guidance, but businesses need to let their suppliers know what their expectations are and when those expectations are not being met. And businesses need to celebrate joint successes with their suppliers. As important as it is for companies to improve quality and customer focus, it is equally necessary for businesses to be more proactive in their partnerships.

It's also important for businesses to face new realities in business relationships. Sometimes they need to forget past mistakes or "wrongs" if there is a genuine effort at improvement. It's true that bad news travels faster than good. If a customer is wronged, they will likely tell 15 others, but if a customer has a great experience, they will likely tell only three others. Customers have a tendency to cling to past impressions when they have had unfavorable experiences with a company.

The problem is if businesses refuse to let go of yesterday's woes, the result could be likened to an anchor dragging from a ship when it's trying to sail. This type of behavior could wind up being a self-fulfilling prophecy, i.e., poor service from the supplier. Naturally, suppliers need to keep focused on meeting and exceeding customer expectations. However, with more proactive customers, the supplier will get there much faster and both the supplier and the customer will come out winners. And that's what partnership is all about! If we all put forth more effort at becoming better customers, the bottom line is we'll all get better services and have better products.

ECONOMIC DOWNTURN STRATEGIES

In an economic downturn, the typical knee-jerk reaction is to cut expenses across the board. Although I agree that there may be some areas where cutting expenses might be prudent, I do believe there are areas where it would be appropriate to resist the temptation to cut. First and foremost, never cut the value to your customers. Home Depot is the poster boy for this. In an economic downturn, they cut the headcount that waited on customers in the stores. What happened to their sales?

There are two expenses that also fall prey to the corporate axe. One is advertising and marketing and the other is training. This is because they are variable expenses and are much easier to cut than other areas. If you had a competitor and you learned that they had cut their advertising and marketing, what might be a prudent thing to do? It may be counterintuitive thinking but it could be a better strategy to increase your advertising. To use a fishing analogy, the competitor took their worm out of the water; perhaps it's a good time to put two worms in. Many companies have increased their market share and sales when they increased their advertising and marketing in tough times.

The second variable expense is training. If you cut training, consider the impact not only on employee morale but also on customer service. Customers really don't want to deal with employees that don't know what they're doing. So perhaps you should try the following counterintuitive thinking strategy. Tell your employees that, even though it's a tough economy, you are investing in them in terms of training so they have the tools to bring more value to the customers in competitive times. When I was a corporate executive, I would cut headcount before I cut training. Would you rather have 100 employees that are not trained versus 95 that are trained? Most companies do not have an account number labeled "the cost of not training" and they don't see the cost of not training quantified in a single account. However, it does hit your P&L. The cost of not training can show up in rework, overtime, lost customers, lower employee morale, and this could result in employee turnover, rush delivery charges . . . and the list goes on.

The counterintuitive thinking strategies to consider are:

Increase the value you bring to your customers.
Find your Third Egg;

Increase your marketing and advertising;

Sponsor more contests for your sales reps and
employees in order to raise the bar;

Increase your investment in training; and

Consider investing in technology that will help
employees add value to customers.

| Account #XXXXX | NOT TRAINING | $$$ Millions |

DON'T CUT TRAINING

Does your company have an account number labeled "the cost of not training"? Too many companies have repeated meetings to rigorously go over the numbers; however, rarely does someone in those meetings say, "What are we missing with regard to training? Why are we not spending more on training for our employees?" They think training will be a hit to their bottom line. But it will definitely be a hit to their bottom line if they don't train their employees.

DON'T CUT ADVERTISING

During World War II, Philip Wrigley, son of the founder and then president, led the company in an unusual move to protect the reputation of its brands. Because of war conditions, supplies of top-grade ingredients became limited. At the same time, the demand for chewing gum increased. Large quantities were supplied to the Armed Forces, since gum helped ease tension, promote alertness and improve morale among the fighting men. The company could not make enough top-quality gum to meet everyone's needs. So rather than change the high quality that people expected in these brands, the company took Wrigley's

Spearmint, Doublemint and Juicy Fruit off the civilian market. By 1944, the entire output of these brands was directed to the U.S. Armed Forces overseas.

That same year the company launched the Orbit brand in the United States as a replacement brand. The company told the public honestly that this product, though pure and wholesome, was not quite good enough to carry a standard Wrigley label. Soon after that, top-grade materials became even more scarce and pre-war quality gum could not be produced even for the Armed Forces. So the company completely stopped making its established brands, and the replacement wartime brand was supplied to the Armed Forces. Meanwhile, a unique advertising campaign continued to keep the name and quality of Wrigley's gum in consumers' minds, even though they couldn't buy it. Dramatic ads featured a picture of an empty Wrigley's Spearmint gum wrapper with the slogan "Remember This Wrapper."

After the war's end, the company was again able to purchase the ingredients used in its established brands. Wrigley's Spearmint came back on the market in 1946; Juicy Fruit followed later that same year and Doublemint reappeared in 1947. Though these brands had not been sold in the United States for two years, they quickly regained and then exceeded their pre-war popularity

What type of counterintuitive thinking does your organization need to use?

.

MINING THE NON-PRODUCT GOLDMINE

Early decline and certain death
are the fate of companies whose policies
are geared totally and obsessively
to their own convenience
at the total expense of the customer.
- Theodore Levett

NON-PRODUCT AREAS ADD VALUE TO THE CUSTOMER

Non-product areas can be a huge opportunity to increase your competitive advantage, but most companies have not looked at non-product areas for opportunities to "add value." Most organizations have focused on the product, support for the product and customer service in regard to the product. This chapter will highlight a plethora of non-product areas that can be used to add value for the customer. I tell every audience I speak for that they should get at least one gold nugget they can take and implement from this material. I challenge each reader to look for gold nuggets in terms of how each of these examples could be applied to your organization.

INSTRUCTION MANUALS CAN ADD VALUE
EXPERIENCE IT YOURSELF...AS THE CUSTOMER

Let's take a look at some of the processes that can help create more value for the customer. Here's an example: if your product has to be installed by the customer, then I suggest you take that product and go through the installation yourself. How many of you have ever sat down at Christmas time with one of your kids' presents and tried putting it together with "simple, step-by-step" instructions? If you've gone through that process, you know exactly what I'm talking about. I suggest that companies take their "simple, step-by-step" instruction manual and have one of their employees go through the installation process, just as a customer would.

> **Rate Your Instructions:**
>
> **A   B   C   D   E   F**

CONTRACTS, FORMS, AND PAPERWORK CAN ADD VALUE

In one of our client organizations, the legal department was engaging in "inside-out" thinking. They wanted to do it their way and didn't think about whether their contracts or forms or paperwork were too cumbersome for customers. When we first met with them they said, "Well, that's just the way it is."

We had to get the legal department to think "outside-in," which meant they had to make the contracts, forms and paperwork easier for the customer. One of the goals was to reduce the amount of pages in the contract so it would be easier for the customer to do business with them. The fundamental premise was to get every single function of the company to focus more on adding value for the customer.

In our experience, this is a potential mother lode of competitive advantage. Because, trust me, the employees in most companies have not thought about how they add value for the customer. If I ask them what their job function is and what it is they do, it's easy for them to respond. But if I ask them, "How do you add more value, compared to whoever has your job over at the competitor's company?" I always get a puzzled look. It's obvious they haven't really thought about it. But when they get to thinking about how they can apply their creative energy to figure out how to add more value for the customer, it is amazing the things they come up with.

CREATE FORMS FROM THE CUSTOMER'S PERSPECTIVE

Several years ago, I walked into a medical office. When I checked in at the counter, the employee asked me if I had ever been there before. I responded, "Yes, several times with my children." She asked me if I had been there before as a patient. I said "No, I haven't." At that point, she gave me a clipboard with a form to fill out, and I sat down to fill out their form.

After looking at it, I walked up to the counter and asked her if I could have another copy of the form. Fortunately, she didn't ask me why I wanted it. The reason was that the very first question on the form was not my name or my reason for coming in; it was, **"Who is responsible for payment of the account?"**

The reason I wanted a second copy of the form was that I was going to be the keynote speaker at a medical convention in three months. I wanted to bring a copy of the form with me so I could demonstrate to the audience why patients sometimes get frustrated with their processes.

The form I held in my hand was another example of "inside-out" thinking. I don't have a problem with being asked who is responsible for payment of the account. But how about not making it the first item on the form? Plus it was the only line **in bold**.

All too often, companies do not think about the impact their paperwork or processes have on the customer. This is because they are "inside-out." Could your paperwork be more "outside-in" and add more value?

WEBSITES

It is my belief that websites are a largely untapped source for bringing value to customers. Think about who designs websites: techies, propeller heads—I was one. Here's the scenario: a techie sits down with senior management and asks, "What do you want on your website?" Neither one of them has a clue what an "outside-in" website means. You have the blind leading the blind.

The typical website starts with the home page—a picture or description of the company and a drop-down menu of the products. You can select whatever product you want and there's a drop-down menu with support and then a "contact us." Average—not Awesome! Typically, companies are all too often greedy and think their website is just about getting more sales. They don't see it as an opportunity to bring value to their customers. I believe this is a huge missed opportunity.

So here's a question: How would your customers grade your website in terms of bringing value to them?

A: **Awesome.** Your website is extremely easy to navigate and provides a lot of value added.

B: **Fairly easy.** A lot of value added.

C: **A lot about the company.** Not much value added and often difficult to navigate.

D: **No value added.** Very difficult to navigate; it's an electronic version of your brochure.

F: **Pathetic.**

I've asked many companies about their website and many have responded, "Our website is pathetic." In good times you should have a good website. In tough times it's even more critical. Your website has huge upside potential written all over it. There are so many average to below average websites. If your competitor has an average website, perhaps this is an opportunity to leap ahead of them by having an awesome website. A website that is "outside-in," easy to navigate, and adds value.

Bottom line: websites are a huge, and often missed, opportunity to "add value" for customers.

Companies have available to them all the latest technology; however, as the saying goes, "Artificial Intelligence is no match for natural stupidity."

Artificial Intelligence is no match for natural stupidity.
- Unknown

Something to avoid is trying to make your website trickier and flashier and using technology for the sake of technology. Doing techie stuff because it's cool needs to be eliminated—get rid of it. Customers are not impressed with a bunch of flashy stuff, particularly if it takes far too long to load. Simple is better. Make sure the customer can navigate easily to the information they want. If the customer can't find what they want quickly, they will click off. The sad part is that the information is probably there; the customer just doesn't know how to find it—so, for them it is not there. Also, it's a good idea to offer simple feedback options for customers.

Example: e-Bags.com is a client of ours. Talk about an awesome company! They certainly meet my criteria, as well as their customers'. While doing a company workshop, attendees learned that many of the people who attempted to buy luggage on their website would click off because the information on that page was not clear enough for the customer to make a decision. One of the topics we talked about was "silent, dissatisfied customers."

Basically, the customer clicked on their website but then went to another website and bought the competitor's product. These same customers never called or wrote a letter to complain. Once workshop participants understood the concept of "silent, dissatisfied customers," this sparked the idea that perhaps they should have a button on every single page of their website to solicit feedback from customers. So now there is a box on every page that says, "How can we improve this page?" They meet every week to review customer comments, and this effort has dramatically increased their sales.

So, here comes the obvious question: How many websites have buttons that the customers can use to give the company feedback on how to improve that web page? What you typically see is "contact us" or "request information." That's Average. If you want to be Awesome, maybe it's time to use your website as a two-way communications tool. You get information to your customers; they get information to you. If you want a good example of this, go to www.eBags.com. Under their "Contact Us" page you will see a section that says, "Have a Suggestion? Tell us what brands you'd like to see, or let us know how you think we can improve." Now that's awesome!

DESIGN YOUR SITE FOR YOUR MARKETPLACE

Target market: senior citizens. A company I spoke to markets their services to senior citizens. I went to their website to get information about their company. When I got to their homepage, I couldn't help but ask myself the question, "What font size is that?" I guessed about 9 point or maybe 10. Does it make any sense to have 9 or 10 point type when you're marketing to senior citizens? This is not awesome. What do you suppose is the age of the techie who designed the website?

133

YOU NEED MORE THAN ONE SITE
IF YOU MARKET TO DIVERSE MARKET SEGMENTS

If your organization markets to diverse market segments, such as a builder that markets to both schools and casinos, a generic website may be a weak or ineffective marketing tool. If a school district superintendent is considering hiring a contractor for a new school and she goes to a contractor's website and sees pictures of casinos, would that immediately prompt her to call that contractor? And others in the customer's organization might ask, "What are you thinking, hiring someone who builds casinos?"

If you market to diverse market segments, then as an absolute minimum, you need to have at least two separate tabs on your website. For example, one for schools and one for casinos. If a customer wants schools, they will read about how this company adds value for schools. They will see pictures of schools and testimonial letters from schools, and perhaps even a streaming video of a principal or school district superintendent talking about the awesome job the company did of building their school. On the other hand, if someone clicked on "building casinos," they would see everything pertaining to casinos.

There are good technical reasons for having two different URLs, but I really don't want to get into that in this book. In our company, we have two different URLs: One of them, www.howardhyden.com, is our website for my speaking services. If anyone is interested in hiring me as a keynote speaker, they can see videos of me speaking, as well as value-added suggestions for meeting planners, etc. On the other hand, if they're interested in our workshops, they can go to the Center for Customer Focus website at www.customerfocus.org to find information about our workshops, etc. There are two separate websites, but there is also a link to go from one to the other.

MAKE SURE THEY CAN FIND YOU

A website doesn't help you as much as it could if it doesn't come up in searches. Raymond Handling Solutions had a website that was "inside-out." In my opinion, there is only one person in the country who truly understands what an "outside-in" website is. His name is Brian, and he is the person who designed our website. Raymond asked for his name and Brian met with them. He showed them that when you googled "Raymond HS," which is the name of their company, a high school in New Jersey showed up. Raymond Handling didn't come up even in the top 20 listings. Brian then googled "forklift distributor

Southern California," and again they didn't show up in the top 20. Then he googled "forklift distributor LA"—LA is Raymond Handling's backyard—and who showed up? A small mom-and-pop company that was a fraction of Raymond's size. Brian showed them what they needed to do in order to come up to the top of any search for these types of products or services.

Since then, Simon Walker. Raymond's VP of Sales, has clearly gotten on the "add value or stay home" bandwagon. He has put several tools on the website that their customers can use, "free of charge," including calculators to calculate the number of pallets.

PUT STREAMING VIDEO ON YOUR WEBSITE
AN INSTRUCTIONAL VIDEO CAN BE A GREAT
MARKETING TOOL

Jay Steinfeld, CEO of Blinds.com, knew from years of experience that his customers didn't like to measure and install his product. Steinfeld's 67-employee company, based in Houston, hired a videographer to make some instructional videos. These videos would teach neophytes everything they needed to know about installing blinds. "It was a haphazard approach, but we knew we had to do something," says Steinfeld.

When Blinds.com made their first video, they used an actress that had the same technical skills as their target customers. This was to demonstrate how easy it was to do the measuring. They intentionally selected a female to portray the role of the customer, because it is typically women who decide they want new window coverings. They also made it clear that if the customer measured wrong, it wasn't a problem. They would redo the order at no charge. The bottom line is, they took all the risk out of ordering to make it safe for their customers.

Steinfeld's team created a YouTube channel for the videos. They sent links to Twitter users who had tweeted about installing blinds. They sprinkled the videos throughout their "Blinds.com" website. Today, the company has a full-time, in-house videographer. They have a recording studio, and the staff writes, produces, and even performs in over 80 helpful videos. They are constantly creating more videos—everything from measuring and installing to product demonstrations that differentiate products and features. "Video-equipped web pages bring in three times more revenue than pages without videos," Steinfeld says. He projects that profits at Blinds.com will be up 20% this year on revenues of $50 million.

Streaming video on the website is a fantastic tool.

GET VIDEO TESTIMONIALS FROM HAPPY CUSTOMERS TO PUT ON YOUR WEBSITE

As I mentioned earlier, Bob Young with PEI hired me to be the keynote speaker at their fall convention in Chicago and subsequently hired me to do three presentations at their convention the following spring in St. Louis.

As I stood by one of the booths in the hallway in St. Louis, Bob greeted me and I said, "Are you awesome?" He smiled. "I hope so, but I know you are because our board decided that we want you to speak at every meeting going forward." My Director of Business Development, Kate, sent a video camera to Bob and asked him if he would do a video testimonial . . . maybe something about the impact it had on the audience. Do you want to take a wild guess what we did with that streaming video?

Putting streaming video from customers on your website can be a huge marketing plus. Let me ask you this: Who is better at tooting your horn, you or one of your customers?

What percentage of websites do you suppose have streaming video of customers talking about the added value that they received from the company? I'll save you the research—it's miniscule. Here's a feel-good question: Do your competitors have streaming video of their customers bragging about them? I doubt it. This has serious upside potential!

Perhaps it is time to play the game at the awesome level by putting streaming video of your customers on your website. Again, remember to do it by market segment. We have streaming video of speech clients on our speaker website, and we have testimonials from companies that we have done workshops for on our company website. Don't miss this huge marketing opportunity. Use streaming videos of your customers tooting your horn.

A WEBSITE SHOULD BRING VALUE FOR THE CUSTOMER

Last summer I hired my son to come home and sand and stain our decks. I went to Home Depot to buy a paint sprayer and I asked the salesman which one he would recommend. I told him, "I'm not a contractor who will use this frequently; I'm going to use it once, maybe twice in my life." He recommended a particular Wagner sprayer. "They have a great reputation," he said. I bought the sprayer and went home. I read the instruction manual and it said that it came with two nozzles, one for oil-based stains and one for water-based. There were two nozzles in the box; one was pink and one was orange. However, there was nothing in the instruction manual that indicated which was which. I went out on the porch and held the nozzles up to the sunlight looking for a possible clue, such as an "O" for oil or a "W" for water-based. No such luck. I went to Home Depot's website, thinking maybe I could look up this sprayer and perhaps there would be something instructional. What are the odds? Companies need to think about the variety of questions customers may have and put that information on their website.

Tip: Ask all of your employees to write down the frequent questions they get from customers. Have a meeting. Talk about how to post information on the website. It might be a PDF. It might be FAQs, or whatever. Remember, you may be asking the customer to call you between eight and five to get answers, but that may not be the time when they have the problem. They may have the problem on the weekend or at night. Also, if the customer can go to your website and get answers to their questions, consider how much time all your employees could save—time they could spend adding value for other customers. That is a win for the employees and a win for the customer.

BUSINESS HOURS

PUT THE "A" TEAM ON THE FIELD
WHEN THEY ARE NEEDED ON THE FIELD

Westrec Marinas is a company that owns 25 marinas. Obviously a marina rents slips to boat owners. What are the busiest weekends of the year for a marina? The holiday weekends: Memorial Day, Labor Day, 4th of July, etc. Before we conducted a workshop on customer focus, who do you suppose was working on the Memorial Day weekend? Was it the ace mechanic, or was it the part-time high school kid who couldn't spell boat if you spotted him two consonants and a vowel? Obviously, it was the high school kid—Average. If you want to play the game at the awesome level, then you need to be "outside-in." When the teams in the workshop got to brainstorming, they came up with a new play and recommended that the "A" team be on the field when the customer wants the "A" team on the field.

Another example is medical emergencies. When do our kids get hurt the most? On holiday weekends. I have trained hospital staff, including physicians.

Here's the question: Do the "A" team physicians want to work on holiday weekends? No. Does it end up being the intern who works? Often it's not the "A" team. If your son or daughter gets injured on a holiday weekend, would you want the rookie physician working or the "A" team?

Tip: Analyze your business. Do you have the A" team on the field when the customer wants the "A" team on the field, or are you average? Better yet, ask your customers when they would like the "A" team on the field.

HOURS OF OPERATION SHOULD MATCH YOUR CUSTOMERS' NEEDS

We were doing a workshop for a heating and air conditioning wholesale distributor. This is a company that sells to contractors. I arrived at 6:30 a.m. and poured myself a cup of coffee. At 6:35, I looked into the parking lot where there was a sign for "Will Call." Will Call allows the contactors' employees to call in ahead of time and have the company pull the part so it's ready when they get there. At 6:35, I counted 19 contractors standing in the parking lot. Will Call opens at 7:00 a.m. What does this data tell you? It told me that they ought to be opening at 6:30 or 6:00.

This is another example of a company causing an increase in cost for the customer. These contractors are being paid and yet they are standing in line, not productive, and not on the construction site. Contractors typically work 6:00 a.m. to 3:00 p.m., or 5:00 a.m. to 2:00 p.m., not 8:00 a.m. to 5:00 p.m. or even 7:00 a.m. to 5:00 p.m. The company stepped it up and is now playing the game at the awesome level!

Companies need to examine their business hours for a variety of departments to see what time they need to be open. When there are rush times or crunch times for the customer, standard operating hours may not provide enough availability. This can be a good time to step it up and have your people be more accessible for your customers. Companies should adjust their hours and level of staffing to accommodate the customers' needs. Summer hours might need to be different than winter hours. During peak periods for the customer, you might need to increase your availability. Too many companies set their hours and expect the customer to walk to the beat of their drum.

TAKE TIME ZONES INTO CONSIDERATION

Companies typically have hours that are geared to their own time zone, but their customers may well be in different time zones. If a company is located in the Central Time Zone, should their customers in California receive any less service than their customers who are also in the Central Time Zone? Obviously, the answer is no, particularly if you want to play the game at the awesome level. It is amazing how many companies operate as though all customers were in their own time zone. It is tough enough thinking about domestic time zones, let alone international time zones.

Professional Compounding Centers of Australia (PCCA) sells to pharmacies across the U.S., as well as in Canada and Australia. While in Australia, Frank Raue, General Manager, indicated to me that there were a number of different time zones in Australia. PCCA was located in Sydney but their customers, the pharmacists, were scattered across the entire country. Some were in Western Australia, which is abbreviated to W.A. However, PCCA's employees often referred to W.A. as "Wait Awhile," meaning if a pharmacist in Wait Awhile ordered product, they best get their order in by 10:30 a.m. Sydney time. Clearly, customers in Wait Awhile didn't get the same level of service as other time zones. Employees at PCCA recognized their business hours as "inside-out," and designed a new play that turned around orders from W.A. with the same speed as those customers in other time zones. It's not hard to see why pharmacists in W.A. no longer feel like second-class citizens.

Do you have customers in different time zones? Do they have to "Wait Awhile" for their products or support, or do they receive the same level of service as those in your own back yard?

In many instances, when employees discuss how the company can open earlier or stay later to better serve the needs of customers, it sparks a discussion about employee hours. It turns out that some employees indicate they would like to start later (and therefore stay later) because they need to get the kids off to school in the morning. Others want to come in earlier and finish earlier so they can be there when their kids get home from school. The issue is that management has never really discussed hours that are convenient for the customers OR the employees. It can be a double win. My experience is that employees can be extremely creative, and therefore it might be best to leave scheduling up to the employees rather than management. Management's role should be to meet with the employees and determine what the optimum hours are to better serve customers. Then, leave it up to the employees to figure out work schedules.

Does your company need to step it up in terms of business hours to add more value?

ORDER ENTRY SYSTEMS
PEOPLE ARE PEOPLE—NOT NUMBERS

Everyone has experienced a company asking for their account number. The worst example of using account numbers is when you dial into a company and the automated attendant asks you to type in your account. Then you manage to successfully navigate through the telephone tree and get to the desired person, for which, I believe, you should win a prize. When you finally get to a live human being, the first thing they ask is, "What's your account number?" All of us are then thinking, "Why did you ask me for that in the first place, if you're just going to ask again?" This is not exactly awesome; average might even be a stretch. My personal response to anybody that ever asks me for an account number goes like this: "Beats the socks off me! The good Lord gave me a certain amount of short-term RAM and in my short-term RAM is my wife's birthday, our anniversary, my PIN number for my bank and my Internet password, and that's about it. I do not have any leftover RAM to memorize your account number."

If a company forces the customer to give an account number before they will interact with them, that company is "inside-out," not "outside-in." In fact, most times when we give our name, it can be looked up just as quickly and easily as a number. I'm not a number! You're not a number! You have to wonder why so many companies treat their customers as though they are nothing more than a dehumanized, numerical computer entry.

One of our clients is Domino's Pizza. Can you imagine calling Domino's and having their employee ask for your account number? When their phone rings, they know where the call is coming from, what kind of pizza you ordered last time, and directions for delivery to your house.

Project numbers can easily fall prey to the same disease as account numbers. Asking for project numbers is another example of "inside-out" thinking—Average. It creates a great opportunity for the competition. Customers want suppliers who make it "easy" to do business with them and they don't want to feel like a number. Another rocket science alert.

PREPRINTED ORDER FORMS

Federal Express sent our company a supply of forms. What was unique about these forms was that they had preprinted our company's name, address, telephone number, zip code and account number. We didn't ask them to do that. They just sent us the forms. Consider the following scenario . . .

One of my employees needed to send something to a client. I said, "Send it overnight and make sure they get it by noon tomorrow." I didn't say, "FedEx it." I just said, "Send it overnight." The question is, "Since we have Federal Express, UPS, Airborne, Express Mail, etc., whose form will my employee pick up?" You guessed it: the Federal Express form. This is an example of adding value, even with paperwork.

BLOW UP BAD ENTRY PROCEDURES

A few years ago, I was hired by a hospital in Long Island. The CEO gave me a heads-up that their number one complaint on a customer satisfaction survey was wait time when you came in for surgery. Let's assume that you are going to have surgery at 9:00 o'clock tomorrow morning. What time do they tell you to show up? Six o'clock. Three hours before surgery. There you are, waiting for three hours in what they call the Registrar Department. Next problem: when they finally call your name, you go to the desk and they force you to regurgitate all the information you gave them a month ago. Let's say that you are a customer of a company on a regular basis. If you call into that company and they force you to repeat information you know they already have, what is your impression of that company? Not too hot. So, rule number one: never, never, never force the customer to regurgitate information that you already have, unless you want to look stupid.

Never, never, never force customers to regurgitate information, unless you want to look stupid.
- Howard

During the workshop, the teams brainstormed on the order entry system, and determined it was "inside-out." Then they had to brainstorm and make it "outside-in." I said, "Don't be the doc; be the patient. Stop being the nurse; be the patient." Now they've designed the system to be "outside-in".

Here's the new play: the whole Registrar Department is gone. The CEO's favorite expression is "Blow it up." The Registrar Department part of the facility is now available to be used for something else; so are the computer terminals. All the registrars are gone. They didn't fire them; they are doing other things.

The form that would have been in the Registrar Department is now on the hospital's website. The patient goes to the website a month before surgery. The form is there with whatever information the hospital already has on file. There is a line at the top that says: "If any of the phone numbers, etc. has changed, please update." So you fill in any changed or missing information. Then when you show up for surgery the first person you see when you walk in is a greeter (a page out of Wal-Mart's playbook).

The hospital now has senior citizen greeters. You walk into the hospital and the greeter says, "Are you here for surgery?" If the answer is "Yes," the greeter asks your name, and then types it into an electronic device. Your information pops up. "Mr. Hallquist, you are in Room 255. May I escort you to your room. . . ." Zero wait time. Now that's an awesome play! Not only does it add a tremendous amount of value, but also what did it cost the hospital? In actuality, it saved them a ton. The order entry process is now "outside-in." Again, zero wait time and no senseless regurgitation of information. Might that spread some PWOM?

USING TECHNOLOGY TO ADD VALUE

We have used technology to track our sales, receivables, inventory, payroll, etc. for decades. We are on the threshold of some very exciting times in terms of using technology to "add value" for the customer. GPS, smart cards, and nanotechnologies are just the short list of technologies many companies are using to bring more value to their customers.

SMART CARDS

Service Directions, Inc. is a company that sells and maintains laundry machines for apartment owners. SDI thought that it was absurd that residents of a building had to horde quarters to be able to do laundry. With market prices rising, the quarter increments irritated customers. Every increase had to be in multiples of 25 cents.

Here's their story: "We started working on smart card technology in the 1990s, but it wasn't until after Howard's workshop that we set a strategic goal to be 100% coinless. We are now 85% coinless and well on our way to reaching our goal.

"There are many benefits of this new system. It enables price increases to be in nickel increments, and allows us to give instant refunds to tenants instead of making them wait for a check in the mail. The use of the Internet has accelerated our effort. It allows the residents to revalue the smart card with a credit card and they no longer have to bring cash or coins into the laundry room. This not only adds to the security of employees who had to collect the cash; it also adds to the security of the building since there is no longer cash in the laundry room. It also reduces the carbon footprint since SDI no longer has to send a collection vehicle to the location. When a customer puts $20 on their smart card, the effect is that SDI is getting payment in advance, so they realize a faster deposit of revenues. Another benefit to SDI is that it reduces losses from break-ins to the laundry machines. For the customer, it eliminates the need to hunt for quarters to do their laundry. This was a win-win."

POINT OF SALE (POS) SYSTEMS

I went to a restaurant with several members of a client organization. When we sat down, the waiter came over and took our drink order. He entered the information into a handheld device and pushed a button. That information went to a receiver somewhere in the restaurant which then recognized it as a drink order and forwarded it to the bar. When the drinks were ready, a signal was sent to the server's device. Then, when he took our food order, he hit a button; it went to the receiver; the receiver recognized it as a food order and forwarded it to the kitchen. When the food was ready, a signal was sent to the server.

Without this technology, the waiter might have gone to check to see if the food was ready. If it wasn't, he might then have waited on a few more tables. Meanwhile, he might have missed the food by a minute or two and the food might sit there getting cold. This technology allows the restaurant's employees to maximize their face-to-face time with customers and also allows them to deliver the food and drinks to their customers as soon as they are ready. This technology is an enabler of adding value to the customer. The employees are spending a higher percentage of time with customers and less time running back and forth.

I believe that we are just on the threshold of some very exciting times in terms of using technology to add value for customers.

VALUE ADDED ACCOUNTING SYSTEMS
– NOW THERE'S AN OXYMORON FOR YOU
(JUST KIDDING)

Are the accounting systems within the company "inside-out" or "outside-in"? Accounting systems can add value.

Example: We are the largest customer of a printing company in Colorado Springs. When we get a new client, our office manager sends the guts of a manual to the printer with a cover sheet that explains how many manuals we want printed. I really don't want to carry a big box of manuals on airplanes. So, rather than have the manuals come back to our office, we have our printer ship them directly to our customer.

When the printer got the account, we explained that he must have 100% on-time delivery. We repeated it...we said, "It must be 100% on-time delivery!" Then we asked, "Did we say 99.9%?" Their rep responded, "No." So our expectation was that the manuals were going to get there every single time. We also communicated the fact that if he ever missed getting them there, we would look for a new vendor; no second chances. I did not want to hear that it snowed and therefore the manuals did not get there. It wouldn't be the first time in the history of the world that it snowed. Nor did I want to hear that United mechanics were doing a worker slowdown, and therefore the plane didn't get the manuals there on time. They must be there 100% of the time; no excuses. We have used this printer for over five years.

> *The customer does not want to give you mulligans . . . get it right the first time. - Howard*

One day I called the owner, whose name is Steve. I hadn't stopped to think what an impact my call would have on him. His first question was, "The manuals did get there on time, didn't they?" I said, "Yes, that's not why I'm calling." I could hear a sigh of relief on the other end of the phone. That's what you call a Maalox moment. Then I said, "I called to talk about your invoicing process. Every day when you get an order from us, you ship the manuals and the next step is that your employee gets in his car and drives to our office. He has our office manager initial an invoice and then he leaves. This happens almost daily." Steve said, "Yes, that's our process." I asked the owner how often I paid my accounts payable. He responded correctly, "Every month."

I'm on a monthly system and he's on a daily system. Is he in sync with the customer? Would it also be fair to assume that Steve is laboring under the false pretense that because he is invoicing his customers daily he is getting his cash quicker? Is that his thinking?

Now, the reason I decided to bring this to his attention is that if he is doing this for us he is probably doing it for all of his other customers. This is raising his costs. If he is raising his costs, who ultimately is paying for that? Also, if we get invoices every day and we are entering them into our accounting system, he is driving up our cost of doing business with him. I told Steve, "I would appreciate getting one invoice with a detailed listing of the various orders each month." In my experience, many companies send an invoice to their customer whenever they ship a product, even when that same customer may order multiple items during the month. They are just adding a lot more expense to their side and a lot more expense for the customer.

DESCRIPTION FIELDS CAN ADD VALUE

Another example of "inside-out" accounting is the description field. Each invoice, besides having the client's name, address and the dollar amount, usually has a description field. The question is, "Are the words in the description field 'inside-out' or 'outside-in'?" Almost always, they are "inside-out." When the customer receives an invoice and they do not understand the terminology in the description field, what do they do with that invoice? They have two choices. They can call and ask you what the invoice is for, using their time to unscramble your accounting mess. Or they simply don't pay it and wait until they are in the "over 90-days" column. Then you're calling them and asking why they haven't paid the invoice yet. Again, the customer is using their time to unscramble your accounting mess. Companies would much prefer to have their employees focusing on adding value for their customers rather than spending all that extra time cleaning up their suppliers' messes. The point is, the description field should be "outside-in." If you want the customer to pay invoices promptly, use words in the description field that make sense to the customer.

Example: Westrec Marinas used an invoice format for its 15,000 customers that was developed by the accounting personnel. It worked really well for the accountants. The problem was, it didn't work well for the customers. The invoice was complicated and nearly impossible to understand unless you were a Westrec accountant. Worse, the front line customer service employees, who had to deal with customer questions and billing issues, couldn't decipher the invoices either. Over the years, customers would grumble every now and then about the "unfriendly" nature of the invoices, but the response was either, "We've always done it this way" or "It's a corporate accounting decision how the invoices read." At which the customer would roll their eyes and go away shaking their head.

I introduced Westrec to the concept of "inside-out" vs. "outside-in." Westrec realized that the company had viewed this issue solely from the accountants' standpoint. They had not been looking at it through the customer's eyes and had not been listening to the customer. They garnered feedback from customers regarding how they would like to see the invoices. Then they set about changing the format, which, by the way, was a simple and inexpensive fix. Once the format was changed, customers provided positive feedback to Westrec. Some even took time to actually write a testimonial letter stating how awesome the new invoices were. Imagine getting a testimonial letter due to an easy-to-understand invoice. Problem solved. Incidentally, not only did the customers find the new invoice format a better product; so did the accountants and customer service employees.

A customer actually wrote on their invoice:
"Your new invoices are AWESOME."

YOUR INVOICE SHOULD MATCH YOUR PROPOSAL

Another example of "inside-out" accounting is when the invoice does not match the amount specified in the proposal. Several of our clients are either engineering consulting firms or some sort of professional organization where they are required to write proposals. When they write the proposal, they lay out their fee structure. Then the question is, "When the client receives the invoice, does it match the amount in the proposal?" In many cases, the two are not congruent. They bid the project one way but billed it another way. This only frustrates the customer. It brings up the question, "Why are you charging me more?" It also slows the whole process down. Once again, the company has a receivables problem and they have to call and hassle the customer. If the invoice had matched the proposal, it would have gone right through the system.

This is called "accounting correct; customer stupid." - Howard

Try this awesome play: tell your customers that they will never receive an invoice from you that is greater than the fee quote, and if they do receive such an invoice, you will eat the difference. Perhaps the job does change and the fees go up. In that case, you send a revised fee schedule based on the changes and get confirmation from the customer. Never, never, never bill customers for more than you bid. I am not interested in giving away money; however, I don't want to make the customer ballistic. If your team knows that you will eat the difference when that happens, they will focus on making sure it doesn't happen.

ACCOUNTS RECEIVABLE AND YOUR INVOICING PROCESS

A company in San Diego had a problem with their accounts receivable. Their number of days in accounts receivable was often in excess of 190 days. This was a huge issue, costing them a lot of money. When they evaluated their invoicing process, the employees were quick to determine that the process was "inside-out." Let's look at the invoicing system through the eyes of the customer. When this company sent an invoice, the customer's accounting department received it. However, the customer's accounts payable person did not authorize it to be paid because the invoice needed to be broken into a variety of different project numbers. Then it was sent to those project managers to make sure they initialed their project number and amount. Then it was sent back to accounting before the invoice was authorized for payment. These project managers were not exactly sitting at their desks waiting to process invoices. They spent the bulk of their time in the field. Initialing an invoice is significantly far down on their priority list. And it took weeks before they all verified the amounts.

In order to convert this to an "outside-in" process, the employees met with their customers and gained an understanding of how they processed invoices. Today, when this supplier sends an invoice, all of the project numbers have been preapproved by each of the project managers. Thus, when the invoice is sent to the client's accounts payable person, all the work is already done. The invoice goes right through the system. The number of days in accounts receivable dropped dramatically. The financial impact of that was estimated to be in the hundreds of thousands of dollars.

CREDIT HOLDS

A heating and air-conditioning wholesaler/distributor sells parts and systems to contractors. Every day they receive calls from the contractor's employees to check and see if a specific part is available. The distributor's employee checks the inventory to make sure the part is there and then responds to the customer by saying, "Yes, we have that part and it will be available for you at 'will call' later today or tomorrow morning."

In one particular instance, when the employee of the contractor came to pick up the part, he was told that his company had been put on "credit hold." About 20 minutes later, the distributor received a blistering phone call from the owner. He was about a ten on the Richter scale. He asked, "You told my employee our company is on credit hold? What were you thinking?" You can imagine the rumor mill taking over with the employee telling other employees that perhaps their company was going under or wasn't financially sound. The contractor was ballistic and for good reason. He told the distributor that his company had been a customer for over 20 years, had always paid bills promptly, and should never have been put on credit hold. The company was highly successful and profitable and there was no risk of the bills not being paid. He was adamant that if he was ever put on credit hold again, he would take his business elsewhere.

Adopt a one-size-fits-all policy and you just might shoot yourself in the foot. Certainly there are customers that should be put on credit hold. And there may be customers that should never be put on credit hold—they have excellent credit, a great track record of paying their bills, and are highly successful. Companies should identify these customers and flag them in their accounting system.

Tip: Have a meeting to brainstorm criteria and which customers should never be put on credit hold. Make sure that the information is in your MIS system and at the fingertips of employees. If one of those customers shows up for a product or service, and they have an unpaid invoice, the customer should be served as usual. Then someone in accounting can be notified to give the customer a call regarding the unpaid invoice.

COMPANY POLICIES

RETURN POLICY: DON'T PUNISH A LOT OF GOOD CUSTOMERS FOR THE BAD BEHAVIOR OF A FEW

Organizations should take a serious look at some of their policies, making sure they don't create stupid hoops for the 99% of their good customers to jump through. All too often, policies are created because 1%, or even one customer, has taken advantage of the organization. Policies to protect themselves against that 1% must be designed in such a way that they don't punish good customers.

Nordstrom has a reputation for having one of the most liberal return policies in the world. They never say a sale is final. Is there any chance that someone might take advantage of their liberal policy? Of course; there's no doubt about it, but they stand by their policy. They say, "We want our customers to shop with confidence, knowing that if there is ever a problem, we will take care of it."

PCCA Australia has a customer that rarely asks for credit, but when he does, he wants the company to take back his unopened stock. The customer has almost always defaced the labels on the bottles. So what PCCA did was reaffirm to the customer their official return policy and credit him for the stock ($80) only. Since their customer had said it was important for him to write on the labels, PCCA sent him a pack of small, blank, removable adhesive labels. Their customer was happy, and the ingredients are still saleable for PCCA to rework and put back into stock.

So the choice is to quote your policy and do nothing for the individual customer, or solve the problem and make it a win for the customer, which will turn into a win for you. You will get WOM. The choice is whether it will be NWOM (Negative Word of Mouth) or PWOM (Positive Word of Mouth).

FORECAST YOUR CUSTOMERS' NEEDS
TRACKING CUSTOMER INFORMATION CAN ADD VALUE

Does your MIS system track just your information or does it track customer information too? Companies need MIS systems to track their sales, expenses, inventory, payroll, etc. The question is, "Do you track customer information?"

THE COMMON APPROACH: "YOU SOLD IT TO ME."

When a customer calls a company from which they have bought a product, an employee on the other end of the phone asks, "What model number do you have?" or "What is the make and manufacturer of the product?" How many customers have thought, "You sold me this product and you don't know what it is?" Another classic example is when the customer calls in for tech support for their computer system and the person asks the customer, "What is your serial number?" The customer now has to get down on their hands and knees or lie on their back and try to find the serial number (which is in micro font and probably not in the best light). This, again, falls in the category of, "You sold it to me; why don't you know the serial number?"

For example: My wife gave me a honey-do note that included fixing the broken handle on the convection oven. I needed to order a new one. I looked inside the oven and outside the oven for the model number; it was nowhere to be found. I am confident that it was probably on a plate on the back. However, I was not about to take the oven out of the built-in wood enclosure. I called the builder and asked for the model number, the manufacturer's name, and an 800 number I could call to get a replacement part. Stop and think for a moment . . . if you called your builder, would they have that type of information at their fingertips? Usually the answer is no.

THE UNCOMMON APPROACH

The supplier's MIS system tracks what products the customer bought. What if the builder recorded all of the following information in their MIS system: the model number and manufacturer for water heaters, air conditioners, furnaces, microwaves, dishwashers and all other appliances installed in the house; the color and manufacturer of the paint for every room in the house; the wallpaper and manufacturer; the color, name and manufacturer of all carpets in the house; the product number of the tile in the house; all light fixtures, etc.? The builder could provide the homeowner with a CD with all this information on it. Or perhaps they could put it on their website and assign the homeowner a username, so at any time in the future a customer could get access to this information. Wouldn't that be awesome? What percentage of builders provide this type of "added value" for their customers?

Some builders reading this might say, "We put together a nice package with the brochures, instruction manuals, etc. and give it to the homeowner." That is Average!

A young man came to my house to repair the dishwasher. As he was working, I was on the phone talking to some of our clients. After a couple of phone calls, he commented, "Whatever you do for a living must be pretty exciting." I told him it was and that I was a keynote speaker on customer focus. He overheard me use the term "Awesome" and he said that was one of his favorite words. When I told him my trademark was "Dare to be Awesome . . . because the rest of the world is Average," he said that is so true. I told him I was going to give him a demonstration of how to play the game at the Awesome level. I also told him that if he did what I was about to show him, he would have a good chance of not only getting a bigger raise than everybody in the company, but he also might become very promotable. He was eager to learn. Obviously I had his attention.

I told him to walk over to the sliding glass doors in the kitchen and look out the windows. I then told him not to turn around as I was asking the questions. I then asked him, "What is the model of the cooktop in our kitchen? What model refrigerator do we have? When you walked through our laundry room, did you notice what model washer and dryer we have?" He drew a blank. I said, "What would happen if you walked into a customer's home and wrote down every appliance the customer had? Then you went back to the company and designed a postcard with a list of all the customer's appliances and sent it to them. And on the postcard you indicated that your company can service all of the listed appliances, and included your company name and phone number. All too often if the homeowner has a Maytag washer and dryer and needs repair service, they will simply go to the Yellow Pages and look for the Maytag logo and call another company. When in fact, *your* company can service that appliance. When you go back to your company, make a mock postcard and document your idea. Documenting the idea will show that you put some thought into it and will ensure that when the company brainstorms on this idea, you get the credit."

This young man was on fire and couldn't wait to get back to his company to implement the idea.

In my experience, employees are constantly walking by opportunities that could result in other sales for their company. A boiler technician should look for other pumps, etc. when they walk through the customer's facility. Perhaps there are other applications for your products or services that represent upside potential. However, most employees are so focused on what they're there for that they miss these other opportunities. If you want to play the game at the Awesome level, the opportunities are there—you just have to spot them.

Opportunity abounds if you want to play the game at the Awesome level. - Howard

DO YOU MAKE IT EASY FOR YOUR CUSTOMER TO DO BUSINESS WITH YOU?

The most obvious way to increase future sales is with your repeat customers. As mentioned in the marketing chapter, getting a new customer is more expensive than keeping a current customer. Add value for the customer by making it easy to work with your organization and customers will keep coming back.

I ran into a gentleman in New Jersey who orders his bicycle tires from a company in Utah. These are not unique bicycle tires; he and his wife both have a mountain bike. We're not talking about Lance Armstrong type bicycles or tires. There are hundreds of places he could buy these same tires in New Jersey.

Why is it that he buys bicycle tires from Utah? When he calls the store in Utah, the employee asks him his name, and then looks it up in the computer. She says, "I see you have a Trek and a Cannondale. Which of your bicycles would you like tires for?" He tells her the Trek. She asks him, "Would you like one tire or two? Would you like next day air, two-day or ground delivery?" This company in Utah maintains the information on what bicycles he has and knows exactly what tires are on those bicycles.

The average process so many companies use is to ask the customer what type of tire they want. How many of us have gone into the garage, got down on our hands and knees, and tried to read the black lettering on the black tire? For this New

Make it easy for the customer. You just might increase sales. - Howard

Jersey cyclist, all that hassle is eliminated because the company in Utah has the savvy to store their customers' information on their computer. A company in Utah is making sales to a customer in New Jersey, selling the same identical tire that's available down the street. You've got to love it when they "get it!"

The majority of companies espouse, "We want our customers to find it easy to do business with us." My experience has taught me otherwise. When employees evaluate their company's non-product areas as to whether those processes are "inside-out" or "outside-in," over 90% are rated "inside-out." When groups of employees get together to design a process, through whose eyes are they looking? Their own. Therefore, the majority of processes default to "inside-out." This is another example of lack of congruence—the processes are not in alignment with the stated values. Companies can't just make these grandiose statements. The challenge is to achieve alignment between what your organization says and how it behaves.

The challenge is to achieve alignment between what your organization says and how it behaves. - Howard

Non-product areas are a dormant source of competitive advantage. When organizations transform their processes from "inside-out" to "outside-in," they are adding more value to the customer by truly making it easier for the customer to do business with them. This is one giant leap from "lip service" to "customer friendly."

Is your organization *really* easy to do business with or are all your processes—like most organizations'—"inside-out"? How many golden nuggets did you find?

Things may come to those who wait, but only the things left by those who hustle. - Abraham Lincoln

INNOVATE OR EVAPORATE

Life is pretty simple:
You do some stuff. Most fails. Some works.
You do more of what works.
If it works big, others quickly copy it.
Then you do something else.
The trick is the doing something else.
- Leonardo da Vinci

ADDING VALUE THROUGH INNOVATION

Innovation is an important part of customer focus. An "outside-in" organization will check in on their customers to see how they are doing. If there is a problem, they will step up and find a solution. The following story is a great example of this.

Occupational Health and Safety, a division of 3M, makes products to keep factory workers safer. One of their products is a mask that covers the nose and mouth to make the respiratory system of a factory worker safer. We've all seen these little masks. The people at 3M decided that it would be a good idea to go out and see how the customer is actually using the product.

Join me now: I want you to picture yourself out on the factory floor. This is an aluminum manufacturing company. Aluminum things are made here. They grind and saw aluminum all day long. There is aluminum dust in the air and all over everything. The masks are in a standard cardboard box and the lid is open. The masks are packed in such a way that the mask is conveniently collecting the dust. If you were a factory worker and you walked over there and picked up an aluminum-dust-covered mask, what would you do with it? Throw it out, right? And the next 3, 4, 5, 6, or whatever it took to get to a clean one.

If 3M were greedy, how might they react to that? "Sales are going up 20%; we're on a roll. In fact, maybe we could figure out a way to make every box stay open—can we make it spring loaded?"

The people at 3M aren't greedy. They are interested in customer focus. They are interested in innovation. Their employees got together and tried to figure out a way to increase the value for the customer. First of all, they packaged each mask in a cellophane wrapper. Then they designed a new box. It is tall and has two columns with a partition down the middle. Now, the customer can simply pull a product out of the dispenser, unwrap it, and apply the clean mask. Does that add value for the customer? Yes. Have they changed the actual product itself? No. The product is still the same. However, the packaging has added value for the customer.

I have been working with "3Mers" over a number of years, and many of them have indicated that 3M is an acronym for innovation; innovation is absolutely critical. Consider the advertising campaign they have had over the years—it features many Olympic athletes. Not just those that have won a Gold Medal but also those who have dared to be different and tried a new technique or a new way to excel.

In fact, at 3M, each of the divisions is required to have a percentage of their next five-years' sales come from products that have yet to be developed. That's right: a full 25% of future sales at 3M will come from products that haven't even been invented yet! How's that for innovation? 3M realizes that if they keep doing the same old things they are likely to fall by the wayside. At 3M, they *cherish* innovation.

WHY CHANGE?

In today's highly competitive market environment, I can't think of a single industry that is not going through dramatic change. The question is, "How do we deal with that change?" To some, it might seem like a problem. I like to think the glass is half full rather than half empty. I'm an optimist and I look at change as an opportunity. Study your customers and the marketplace and figure out what's changing. Become a student of your customer and your customer's business. Figure out what's changing in their business so that you can adapt your products and services to meet those changes. That's using a preemptive marketing strategy. You preempt the competition, because you figure out the "what's changing" and get there first. This strategy can give you a tremendous competitive advantage.

Customers' expectations are going up dramatically. Today's customers are more sophisticated; they have access to more information and with technology they can get access to as much information as they want. They have more choices because there are more competitors than ever before. If you don't do it right, if you don't do it their way, they can go down the street and find somebody else that will sell them what they are looking for.

This year's Awesome is next year's Average.
- Howard

So the bottom line is, the customers' expectations are higher this year than last year and next year they will be even higher. The customer is going to raise the bar next year and demand more value.

An interesting question to ponder is, "What is going to happen to those organizations that milk the status quo and refuse to change?" Even if you're an "A" player in your marketplace today, refuse to change and the customer's expectations are going to leave you by the wayside.

If you come to a bend in the road, it's not the end of the road... unless you fail to make the turn. - Will Rogers

There are numerous examples of companies that fail to respond to change, that fail to respond to the customers' changing needs. General Motors, Kodak, and the list goes on. . . . These were the pillars in their particular industry; they were the best; they were number one and they knew it all. Of course, they didn't need to change. Expertise or success can be an asset. However, it can easily become a liability. In other words, it can blind you to the need for change.

DON'T SIT ON YOUR MERITS— SOMEONE WILL PASS YOU BY

There is a philosophy of yesterday: "If it isn't broken, don't fix it." Today the philosophy is, "If it isn't broken, fix it anyway." Seiko (a joint Japanese and American company) came out with a no-moving-parts digital watch. Within one year of introducing this digital technology, 17 Swiss watch companies went bankrupt! Now hang onto that number for just a minute, and let's play some Trivial Pursuit. Turn the calendar back about 25 years and consider this: what was our perception in the marketplace of the quality of a Swiss watch 25 or so years ago? Outstanding! Magnificent! The best! If you had a Swiss watch, you had the finest watch made. Guess what? That was their liability. It blinded them to see the need for change.

Your strength is your asset; but your strength can easily become your liability. - Howard

What country in the world do you suppose invented the no-moving-parts technology? Was it the Americans or the Japanese? It was the Swiss. Now here's an example of "loose lips sink ships." The employees from the Swiss manufacturer that invented this technology went to a trade show. At this trade show there were employees of a company called Texas Instruments. There were also some employees from a Japanese company. The Swiss employees talked about the no-moving-parts technology but said, "That's not where the marketplace is. This is a watch. It's got gears, pendulums, etc. We put the digital technology on the back burner." Well, the employees of Texas Instruments and the Japanese company got together and formed a joint venture; the joint venture was called Seiko. Seiko introduced the no-moving-parts technology and "Bingo!" Within one year there were 17 Swiss watch companies in bankruptcy. That's the price of "We're number one! We're the best! We're awesome and we don't need to change."

When I hear the words, "We've always done it that way," I think of disease. Companies should be focusing on continuous improvement. Consider this for a minute; if you are not willing to take the risk, it is unlikely that you will reap the rewards. Can you steal second base if you keep your foot firmly planted on first? Continuous improvement means we need to learn to take risks and not fall into the "We've always done it that way" mindset.

Consider the printing industry. For decades, the printing industry has printed the newspapers, magazines and books and then distributed them by shipping the finished product. Now that is rapidly changing, and you can read newspapers, magazines and books online. Printers that don't keep up with new technologies and don't see the new opportunities are going to be left by the wayside.

Asking the Right Questions Can Uncover Added Value

Sometimes, I like to talk about coloring outside the lines. When we were in elementary school, one of the rules was to color inside the lines. Today it may be more appropriate to break that rule. Break traditions, dare to do things differently and color outside the lines.

Now let me give you a sample of what I'm talking about. My mother was the kind of parent that if I didn't get straight A's, I was grounded. So, when I came home with a C in algebra, the next thing I knew, I was enrolled in summer school. Let me tell you, I was not a happy camper! Mom was ruining my life. All the other kids were going to play ball or whatever, and I was going to go to summer school. Since I didn't have an option, I decided that I would make the best of it. You know, really nail it. Then next year I wouldn't have to go to summer school. I went to class, studied hard and thought: *All right, I've got all the right answers now.* When the fall semester comes and I'm sitting in that class, my arm is going to be spring-loaded. I am ready. Let me tell you what happened. The teacher changed the questions. I had all the right answers, but they were the wrong questions for my answers.

Consider this: Is that what is happening in your marketplace? Do you have all the right answers to all the wrong questions? The problem is: the customer is changing the questions all the time. Their marketplace is changing.

Let me give you an interesting philosophy that hockey's living legend, Wayne Gretzky, "The Great One," used:

Most people skate to where the puck is; I skate to where the puck is going to be. - Wayne Gretzky

In other words, anticipation is absolutely critical. He skated to where the puck was going to be and that is one of the primary principles that made him "The Great One." Perhaps we can take a lesson and do that in our businesses.

Is your company skating to where the puck is or where it's going to be?

LEARNING WHERE THE PUCK IS GOING TO BE

A good way to find out "where the puck is going to be" is to ask your customers. Dick Gasper was president and chief executive officer of NorthStar Print Group. He had been with the company for three years and had a good grasp of its operations and key markets.

NorthStar is a major label company supplying products to companies like Miller Brewing Co., Procter & Gamble, and Exxon Mobil. Established in 1947, NorthStar had a good reputation as a label supplier. However, it was having difficulty growing business and expanding into new markets. As a result, sales and profit goals were not being met.

A strong advocate of the integrated approach to customer focus, Mr. Gasper had worked with me to successfully reposition NorthStar's pressure-sensitive label division as a "high value-added" label supplier. His main goal now was to use the same customer-focused approach to improve their performance and position the company for future growth.

To gain a better understanding of the best strategic direction for his business, Gasper worked with me to develop a survey instrument that would identify what was important to NorthStar's customers and how they perceived NorthStar. Gasper was looking for ways to add value to NorthStar's products and services and pinpoint specific areas for improvement. He also wanted to find out how NorthStar compared to their competitors.

Analysis of the initial survey data clearly showed that NorthStar Print Group's customers were looking for label suppliers who could help them effectively differentiate their products in the marketplace. Labels are a highly visible component of a product's packaging and play a vital role in marketing and promotion of the product. According to the survey, NorthStar's customers and prospects placed considerable value on working with an "innovative label" provider, one that could suggest new ways for them to increase their products' "shelf impact" and thus sell more product. They were also hoping to reduce label costs.

While NorthStar was already recognized for its product quality, it ranked much lower in "product innovation." What's more, its competitors were seen as being much better at providing customers with new ideas, new products and new label technology.

Like all products, labels have a finite life cycle. As customers' needs change, companies look for new label products that meet those needs. Because NorthStar was not perceived as being innovative, companies would turn to its competitors for the new label products they needed.

NorthStar Print Group was at a crossroads. It could continue to do what it had always done and gradually become less and less competitive, or take the alternative route: develop the ability to provide the type of innovative new label products their customers were looking for. The choice was clear.

Working closely with NorthStar's executive team, we were able to develop a strategic plan that would reposition the company on the leading edge of label innovation. They began to allocate resources to new product development, and they aggressively gathered information on the type of products and services customers were looking for. They also gathered information on the new products being developed by competitors.

As NorthStar worked to establish a base for new product development, it became clear that more work was needed. We refined the strategic plan. To become a market leader, NorthStar would have to begin the development of its new products *before* its customers recognized the need for those products. To do that, they strengthened their working relationship with major customers.

NorthStar also recognized that it did not have all the resources necessary to develop new products on its own. To address this issue, they developed strategic relationships with suppliers. Today, these relationships help NorthStar keep abreast of the latest supplier developments and give them access to the suppliers' product development processes. When appropriate, NorthStar partners with a supplier to develop innovative products that benefit their customers and ultimately their customers' customers.

IF A CUSTOMER HAS A PROBLEM, FIRST IDENTIFY THE PROBLEM

The core element of any marketing strategy I have developed comes straight from the advice of my father so many years ago: "Don't worry about what you can take from organizations or customers; instead, focus on what you can contribute. Don't be the taker . . . be the giver." Concentrate on bringing more value to your customer. Don't act like the king . . . act like the servant. (By the way, this is also not a bad philosophy to adopt in our personal lives.) Those organizations that are zealots at creating value for the customer and empower their employees to execute the strategy with passion are winners, and they have the bottom line to prove it!

There is a company that makes supplies and sells them to hospitals. An astute sales rep calling on a hospital noticed that the nurses were putting two hospital gowns on a patient instead of one. Now, we all know what the problem is here. You're going down the hall after surgery and you're mooning the world. Embarrassing, right? This brings new meaning to the acronym "ICU" and the phrase "the end is in sight."

It's difficult to put a gown on from the rear when you've had surgery. You have stitches . . . you're trying not to bend . . . it's painful. So the nurses in this hospital have to help the patients put on another gown from the rear. Now if you are greedy, you might just think, "Great, that drives up our sales." However, this astute rep looked at the situation as a problem for the customer.

This rep also made another observation—there was a hole in the left side of the gown. Why? Because the nurse had to rig up an IV for the patient, but there wasn't a hole in the gown, so she made one with scissors. She had also made a hole in the right side to rig up the device that dispenses medication. Now, the gown has been laundered about 50 times and was looking pretty shabby. So here's the scene: you've got a patient looking shabby in the front and mooning the world from the back.

The sales rep brought the gown back to the company with the idea that this was an opportunity for the company to add value for the customer. She shared it with the president and the other employees and they agreed that the company needed to modify the design of the gown. Now the patient can still put the gown on from the front but it goes all the way around the back and is fastened with Velcro. The patient is no longer mooning the world. There is also a buttonhole in the upper left front, which works perfectly for the IV, and the right side has a pocket that is just the right size for the medication dispenser. Now *that* is Customer Focus.

Does the new gown bring more value to the customer than the competitor's gown? Of course the answer is "Yes." Who do you think hospitals will want to make future purchases from—companies that sell "average" gowns, or this company, that sells "awesome" gowns? Second question: could they charge more for the new gown? Because their gown brings more value to the customer than the competitor's gown does, the answer, again, is "Yes."

All frequent flyers share a common frustration. We cannot find an electrical outlet with which to charge our cell phone or laptop. If we do find one, someone else has beaten us to it. Can you relate to this? Clearly, whoever designs airports is inside-out. Perhaps it's my engineering background that drives me to solve problems. When I travel, I never need to look for an unused outlet. I simply look for someone who has already found an outlet. I carry a three-way adapter in my computer bag, so I walk up to someone who is already using an outlet, hold out my three-way adapter, and ask, "Would you mind sharing the outlet with me?"

Somewhat stunned, they say, "Sure." Then they say, "What an awesome idea!" When I shared this with a group of CEOs that know me well, they said, "This is vintage Howard; this is how you think. While the rest of the world whines about not being able to charge their electronic device, you solve the problem. You should put your logo on the plug." Since I frequently give one away during my presentations, consider it done.

I gave one to Mark Olson, President of APG Cash Drawer. Mark's company was about to attend a trade show for their industry. Many of APG's customers, as well as potential customers, were also going to attend. APG had a suite where they wanted to attract customers and prospects at this event. Mark asked for our permission to use the three-way adapter idea and print APG's logo on the plug. They then mailed an adapter, with an invitation to visit their suite, to every customer and prospect. Mark said, "It was a huge hit." Many at the event asked if they could have another plug or two or three. Mark happily obliged. Mark "gets it"—big time. Is APG generating any word of mouth? The PWOM engine at APG keeps on chugging and Mark keeps on smiling.

I am continuously amazed at how many companies survive in spite of themselves. I can only conclude that either there isn't a competitor that plays the game at the awesome level or that customers have been trained to accept mediocrity! The momentum of mediocrity in these companies can only last until someone dares to be awesome . . . and raises the bar. Carpe diem—Seize the day!

Professional Compounding Centers of America (PCCA) is a membership-based organization that provides independent compounding pharmacists the fine chemicals, equipment, training and education, and pharmacy and marketing consultation necessary for running their practices. Since it was founded in 1981, PCCA has been known in the industry and among its members for maintaining a strong family atmosphere and experience, providing its members with personal attention and service. However, by its 25th anniversary in 2006, PCCA's staff and membership had grown considerably, and members began to voice concerns that the personal touch they looked forward to from PCCA was being lost.

This is why many teams who win the Super Bowl or World Series do not repeat as champions. Perhaps they believe they are the champions and deserve to win and expect to win. However, they don't have the work ethic and the commitment to training and improving that they did the year they won the championship. Meanwhile, are the other teams shooting to equal the performance of last year's champions, or are they shooting higher? It's the same in business. Competitors are trying to knock off last year's winners. They are raising the bar. In addition, customers raise the bar every year and expect suppliers to bring more value. Raising the bar should be a never-ending part of your organization's culture. Never stick with the status quo or you will be left behind.

PCCA executives began looking for new ways to engage their members that would benefit the customers' pharmacy compounding practices, but also create a deeper connection between PCCA and those customers. Their goals were to enhance the member experience, create value for the members, and build member loyalty.

1.   Concierge Compounding

A pharmacist who was a longtime PCCA member approached the company with a proposal for a program designed to place members in best practice sharing groups in order to help them grow their practices more expediently than if they were doing it on their own. The goals of the program were to enhance communication and growth for both the participating member pharmacist and PCCA, and to foster the sharing and networking culture of compounding that PCCA had created more than 25 years earlier. PCCA's executives were so impressed with the proposal that they hired the pharmacist to implement and oversee the program, which was dubbed PCCA Concierge Compounding.

The basis of Concierge Compounding is peer-to-peer consultation facilitated by PCCA. Members may apply to participate in the program and those chosen must: demonstrate a willingness to share information with the group; be open to new and innovative ideas; have a desire to grow his/her compounding practice; have a strong commitment to meet via teleconference monthly and actively participate in the meeting; and have a commitment to PCCA. Those chosen are assigned to groups of 12 people, and care is taken to delegate the groups to provide geographic diversity so that members are not being asked to share proprietary information with a competing compounder in the member's area.

Every month, the members of each Concierge Compounding group meet via teleconference to share their mutual knowledge and discuss new and innovative therapies available in the compounding arena. They also are given the opportunity to meet face-to-face at PCCA's annual International Seminar, and this has proved to be a popular feature. Members enjoy meeting in person after a year of getting to know the others over the phone! Participants have responded well, and their spending with PCCA has increased since entering the program.

It is one of the most beautiful compensations of this life that no man can sincerely try to help another without helping himself. - Ralph Waldo Emerson

2.   Member Rewards Program

PCCA went "outside-in" to discover what their customers really wanted from their membership. They interviewed a cross section of members, conducting focus groups and one-on-one interviews over the telephone and face-to-face. This input from the membership led to the creation of the Member Rewards program. The program was designed to thank members for their loyalty and show appreciation for their commitment to PCCA.

When interviewed, members asked for more tools to help grow their businesses. They wanted greater access to marketing assistance and educational opportunities. Therefore, the Member Rewards program consists of discounts on marketing materials and educational programs. The program runs on an annual basis and the reward level of Silver, Gold, Platinum, or Diamond is based on the member's total purchases from the previous calendar year. For example, if a member's purchases in 2009 qualified for Gold-level rewards, then the member enjoys those benefits throughout the 2010 calendar year.

Depending on the member's Reward level, they are given a certain percentage discount on the marketing materials PCCA sells to help members promote their businesses. All Reward members are given free educational CDs or DVDs. Members also receive discounts on educational events such as seminars, symposiums, and training classes. Platinum and Diamond members are eligible to receive free admission to educational events and are given access to a dedicated customer service team, which is trained to handle their needs.

Education for customers can be a significant added value. - Howard

The program is now in its third year and has been a roaring success. The total value of the rewards redeemed on educational events in 2009 was more than a quarter of a million dollars, but by giving members the tools to grow their businesses, a cycle begins in which the members are able to reinvest their increased profits with PCCA, which in turn helps PCCA grow its business.

3.   Advisory Council

Customers want to feel valued by the company. They want to feel that their requests and suggestions are heard and to see results. When PCCA conducted focus groups among its members, the results were so successful that senior management decided to take the idea of focus groups and turn it into an ongoing program. The Advisory Council was created to be a strategic thinking body, a sounding board for new PCCA initiatives related to members.

The primary goal for the council is to help PCCA listen to the needs, wants, and challenges of its members so that PCCA can stay one step ahead and better serve its membership. The Advisory Council consists of 12 members who are selected based on qualities such as: having an interest in helping PCCA meet the diverse needs of its growing membership; being a good representative for PCCA; and being a leader with a strong sphere of influence. Each member serves a two-year term on the council.

The Advisory Council has been responsible for a number of successful innovations, including major changes to the format of PCCA's annual International Seminar. Council members suggested that PCCA offer more diverse educational opportunities, so now programming tracks are offered on technical aspects of compounding as well as tracks on business concerns and marketing. The Seminar's new format was well-received in its first year, a victory for the Advisory Council. Their feedback will give PCCA a continually fresh perspective on their members' needs.

The man who says, "it can't be done," is liable to be interrupted by someone doing it. - Anonymous

Is your organization extrapolating what you did last year or do you have specific plans to raise the bar and bring more value?

Excel at the Crisis

The pessimist sees the difficulty in every opportunity.
The optimist sees the opportunity in every difficulty.
- Winston Churchill

This chapter is filled with examples where a company was up against a crisis and then turned things around, or where a company saw an opportunity and went for it. In most cases, when a company's performance shines, it is due to the discretionary effort of their employees.

Learn from Your Customer When Things Go Wrong

Picky customers are much more useful than the silent dissenters. To kick off a workshop for the employees of a tree care company, the CEO played a tape. It was a voicemail he had received from a very upset customer. The company is in the business of caring for trees; they have residential customers and commercial customers. A customer had told the sales rep to make absolutely sure that when the employees came to work on her trees, they did not drive the trucks on her lawn.

Obviously, the employees that had come to do the work had driven on the lawn. The customer was ballistic and when she called the CEO of the company she left an irate message. Some of the employees had labeled this customer as "the picky customer." I asked the group, "Is she really 'the picky customer' or is it possible that she is your most valuable customer? The reason you drove the truck on the lawn was because it was the *exception*. Perhaps instead of looking at her as a picky customer, you should look at her as your *best teacher*. She is showing you how to raise the bar to play the game at the awesome level and you are discounting her." I then asked, "Can you identify six picky customers?" They responded affirmatively. I said, "Perhaps you should invite them all to a meeting." That comment got some very strange looks. "At the meeting, tell them that they are your high expectation customers and that you would like to get their input. Would this help you play the game at the awesome level?"

Create two flip charts, one titled, "Things we should do" and a second titled, "Things we should not do." Then write down exactly what those "picky customers" tell you. Once you have a list of these items, make them your new standard. The "picky customers" tell you how to raise the bar and play the game at the awesome level. In fact, they are not "picky customers"; they are your MVPs (most valuable players) and your best teachers.

Tip: Send a very, very nice basket of fruit and cheese to those "picky customers" to thank them for their input. Thank them for helping you "raise the bar."

Did this company learn from the crisis? In fact, they excelled at the crisis and raised the bar at the same time.

Could your company learn and excel from a crisis?

PANIC CALL FROM THE CUSTOMER

A company that makes equipment for emergency vehicles, police cars, etc., had a problem. One of the sales reps mentioned that there are times when the customer has broken equipment and they are in a real panic to get it fixed immediately. He also indicated that there are penalties associated with not being able to do that. During the discussion, he said, "Wouldn't it be great if we could just turn that thing around in one day and ship it back RUSH? We could save the customer a ton of money."

During one of our workshops, the teams brainstormed and came up with a suggestion. Here's the play they designed: they are going to install a light on the ceiling of the production floor. When a sales rep calls in and has a customer in a panic situation, the light will be turned on and so will a siren. When the preassigned "swat team" of five top employees sees the light and hears the siren, they will drop what they are doing and start working immediately on the emergency equipment order for the panicked client.

The next suggestion was that the company should take a picture of the employees with the finished rush order and send the picture, along with a thank you card, to the customer, saying they were glad they could help them in their time of need.

The teams also discussed the price of this rushed equipment. Would they charge the normal price, or would they be able to charge a premium price based on their awesome response time? When the sales rep gets the panic call, they can say, "We can get the new emergency equipment to you at the normal price and within our normal lead time. Or, if you are in a pinch and it will cost you a lot of money waiting for the product to get there, we can put a rush on it. We can probably get it shipped to you today, and you'll have it tomorrow morning. The cost would be . . . . " Then the rep can explain what that premium price is based on.

So now the customer has a choice. To turn something around in this short time frame is absolutely unbelievable and an awesome play for the customer. It's also a win for the employees. Previously, employees looked at a rush job as a major inconvenience and usually the customer was left waiting. Now, when the light starts flashing and the siren goes off, an excitement erupts throughout the factory floor. The regular employees give the swat team a high five for responding well to the situation, and all the employees have a tremendous sense of pride.

Another plus: think about what it might mean to the sales rep when he's talking to new prospects that know they might find themselves in a similar panic situation. They will know this company is ready to stand up and be awesome. Now that's added value that will give this supplier a competitive advantage. Have they excelled at the crisis?

WHEN THE CUSTOMER THROWS YOU A CURVE BALL...

I was scheduled to speak at Lake Tahoe from 8:00 to 9:00 a.m. When I arrived and looked at the program, I noticed that I had been moved to the 10:30 to 11:30 time slot. The problem was, I had a noon flight out of Reno and there were no later flights I could take. I checked my contract and it said 8:00 to 9:00. When I approached the meeting planner, she explained there had been a change to the agenda. However, no one had communicated this to my office. When I told the meeting planner I had a noon flight, her face got flushed. I told her not to worry; I would work on solving the problem.

I called my office to ask them to find out if there was a helicopter service between Lake Tahoe and Reno. The answer was no. Then I asked them to call the Chamber of Commerce and find out if there was a company that used helicopters as part of their day-to-day operations. There was a company that used helicopters to inspect power lines. We got the president's name and phone number and called him. I told him I was a keynote speaker in Tahoe on the subject of customer focus, and that he could get some great publicity by coming to my aid. I asked him how much he would charge to pick me up in Lake Tahoe and take me to Reno. The answer was $100.

Next we had to figure out a place for the helicopter to land and pick me up, since there was no commercial airport for helicopters near the hotel where I was speaking. The president told me to go to the Ponderosa Ranch, where they had filmed Bonanza. It was only two blocks away, but the timing needed to be exact since what we were about to do was a tad illegal. I told him that I would arrange for a taxi to take me directly to the Ponderosa.

I finished my speech at 11:30. When I told the audience I had a noon flight out of Reno, their looks communicated, "You're screwed." I did not see my taxi driver; however, the audience indicated that he was behind the stage and I thanked them. I jumped in the taxi, and we were at the Ponderosa in three minutes. The helicopter had just landed. I boarded and we flew to the Reno airport. The pilot landed the helicopter on the tarmac and indicated that I should go through the administrative building he was pointing to, make a left, and I would be right at the gate. I thanked him and he took off.

As I walked toward the administrative building, several security guards approached me and asked what I was doing landing a helicopter there. I said, "Well, I didn't land the helicopter, he did." I pointed to the helicopter. "Oops, he's already taken off." I continued to walk because I thought if I stopped, they might not let me continue. The guards said the building was a secured area, and I replied, "I really don't want to see anything of a secure nature. Therefore, I'd be happy to close my eyes if someone will take me by the arm and guide me out the other door. All I want to do is get to the gate so I can board my flight." They looked in amazement, then they guided me through the building and I thanked them. I was now at the gate. It was 11:45 and I boarded the plane 15 minutes prior to departure. The only decision at this point was whether I wanted a beer right then or after I was in the air. By the way, this was before 9/11.

What's the point of the story? Occasionally a customer will throw you a curve ball. Although it may at first appear to be impossible, with a little ingenuity, "impossible" can mean that it just takes a little longer than normal to figure it out.

If the customer throws you a curve ball, it's time to hit it out of the park. - Howard

Another point: Who said that your organization has to screw up before you are allowed to do something special for the customer? If the customer throws you a curve ball, it's time to hit it out of the park.

A CUSTOMER'S PROBLEM CAN BE AN OPPORTUNITY

While waiting to board a flight from Minneapolis to Orlando, I observed a member of the Northwest crew animatedly speaking with the gate agent about the plight of a small boy already on the plane. It seems little Daniel had celebrated his birthday at Disneyworld the day before and was proudly wearing his treasured pirate hat from his visit but was in tears because the eye patch was missing. The crewmember hoped to locate the lost patch in the area where Daniel had been sitting. She was soon joined in her search by the captain and the co-pilot, but the patch was not found.

As I boarded, I noticed Daniel standing tall in the cockpit, along with his sister in her Daisy Duck hat, as the crew made every effort to comfort him. Daniel and his sister were presented with their Northwest wings and then returned to their seats. When only a few minutes were left before takeoff, the co-pilot returned to the waiting area to make one last futile check for the little pirate's eye-patch. A surprise awaited him when he reboarded the plane; Daniel's mother had been conducting her own search and found the missing patch in the bottom of a plastic bag. The co-pilot announced to those around him, "Now we're prepared for takeoff," and gave Daniel a thumbs-up.

What we witnessed in this incident was more than people rallying to help a crying child. It was an excellent example of Northwest adding value to its service by helping a small customer with a problem. Although it was not Northwest's problem, their employees were there to help. In the process, they created a feeling of good will toward Northwest among a lot of other passengers. I firmly believe that problems with customers, when they are handled well, represent opportunities to build business. What type of WOM will this generate?

In a crisis situation, your employees have a choice. They can erode your competitive advantage by being indifferent to your customers—and this will drive your customers away as fast as your marketing efforts bring them in. Or your employees can be empowered and energized to go on the offensive and use their discretionary efforts to go the extra mile when the customer has a problem. When employees come to a fork in the road, they can choose the extra mile or they can choose to give the customer the usual litany: "I'm sorry, but I can't help you. We're not prepared for this kind of thing." How often, when you are a customer, do you hear the words: "it's not my job" or "they won't let us do that" or "the company policy is this" or "I can't because I'll have to check with my boss or the regional manager."

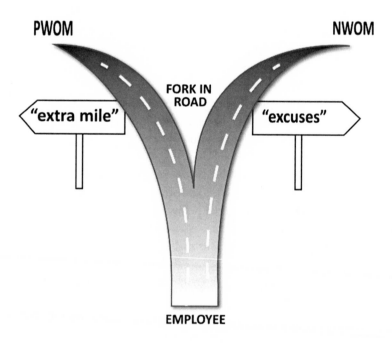

Quality Travel:
"I Need to Differentiate from the Competition"

Here is an example where a company really went the extra mile. An entrepreneur, Frank Martin, had bought the company Quality Travel; he had never owned a travel company before. He called me on the phone and said, "Howard, I need to differentiate myself from the competition. I want to create a 'Wow experience.'" I said, "Frank, what's a 'Wow experience'?" He said, "Simply this: when a customer has a problem and calls us, after they hang up the phone I want them to say, 'Wow! Do you believe that?'"

I said, "I got it." We trained his employees, and here's what happened: Frank landed a new account in central Wisconsin for business travel. He got all the preferences of the people who would be traveling: whether they liked aisle or window seats, etc. He put all the information into the computer. However, the first time this new account was going to use Quality Travel it was not for business; it was for pleasure. The president of the company, his wife, and their two dogs were going on vacation to Boston. No problem. Frank got them tickets, a rental car, a hotel—a terrific travel package. Then they flew off to Boston on vacation.

When it was time to come home, however, the president of the company was going up the coast on business for a couple of days. His wife and the two dogs were going to return home to central Wisconsin. This was in August, and on this particular day, Boston set a record for heat and humidity. The lady got to the airport and went to check in at U.S. Air. The gate agent at U.S. Air said, "I'm very sorry, ma'am. We can take you, but not the dogs. You see, we've got record heat and record humidity."

Can't you just picture this employee justifying in her mind that there's nothing she can do about this; after all, it's an act of God! She offered no solution to the customer with regard to the problem of the dogs' transportation.

Now, put yourself in the customer's shoes. What is she going to do? She knows that she can get on the plane, but is she going to get on the plane and leave the dogs behind? Will she just tell the dogs, "Sorry guys. Hang around the airport. Better luck tomorrow"? No way.

Frustrated, the customer calls Quality Travel and explains the scenario to a young travel agent. The agent says, "I don't know what I'm going to do, but I'm going to do something." She calls several airlines. Finally, she gets to Northwest. Northwest says, "Tell you what. We'll take the dogs, but we'll only take them under the following conditions:

1) The owner has to be on the same flight. We can't have
the dogs showing up with nobody to babysit them.
She has to be on the same flight so she can take
them off our hands on arrival.

2) The owner must sign a release. If those dogs get sick, we don't need a multimillion-dollar lawsuit."

The young agent at Quality Travel seizes the moment. She says, "No problem. We can do it." Now she knows that she can get the woman and her dogs from Boston's Logan airport to Minneapolis, MN. The problem now is that the connecting flight between Minneapolis and the town in central Wisconsin where the customer lives is a Metro Link. That means it's a tiny little aircraft without a pressurized baggage compartment. The dogs can't ride in there because it would kill them.

Now, rather than give the woman the news that she had struck out, the travel agent runs down the hall, grabs a couple of other employees and says, "Help me brainstorm. We've got to figure something out." One of the young employees says, "You know, we use this limo service. Why don't we call them and see if they can help?"

When they dial up the limo service, the guy on the phone says, "Well, we're not in the business of transporting animals. Is this a very important customer?" The young travel agent says, "Well, you see, over here all our customers are very important. It's not a select few, not just our favorite one or two, but each and every customer is very important."

The limo driver says, "Well, I guess in that case, perhaps we can pick her up from the Minneapolis airport in a limo and drive her and her two dogs to central Wisconsin." The young travel agent calls the customer back, and the woman is elated. Can you imagine how relieved you'd feel if you were in her shoes?

There's no speed limit on the extra mile.

Now let me describe the scene at the Minneapolis airport. The customer gets off the plane, and there's the driver and the general manager of the limo service standing there with a sign saying, "Welcome, Mrs. Swensson." Technically they don't need the sign. Why? Because they've called ahead and gotten a physical description of the customer—how tall, what color hair, what color eye glasses, what she's wearing, etc. They couldn't have missed her on a bet. But it's still a nice touch to have the sign.

The woman gets off the plane, sees the sign, and walks over to them, grinning. The general manager introduces himself and the driver and says, "The driver will take you down to the baggage claim to greet your dogs. By the way, your dogs will be coming out Door B."

Now, how did these guys figure this out? They got to thinking. They decided that it was unlikely that the dogs would come sliding down the chute with the rest of the baggage. The dogs will have to come out somewhere else. They called Northwest and said, "We've got a customer coming in on flight so-and-so with two dogs. Could you please tell us where the dogs will come out?" Northwest said, "Sure, just a minute." The employee looked it up and said, "Go down by the baggage claim area. Behind the carousel there's a series of doors. One is marked Door B, and that's where the dogs will come out."

The general manager told the woman, "My driver will take you down to Door B. The second the dogs come out, you'll be there to greet them. I have to go out to my car, but I'll meet you down there in a couple of minutes." The customer and the driver go to the baggage claim area, and the general manager goes to his car. He comes back to the baggage claim area three minutes later with two bowls of fresh water for the dogs.

Does that add value to the customer? But we're not through adding value yet. The general manager takes out a little brown bag. What's inside? You guessed it. Dog biscuits! But we're still not through adding value. The general manager said, "We got to thinking about your dogs. That's a pretty long flight from Boston to Minneapolis, about three and a half hours. The dogs were probably pretty cramped up in their cage. So, we decided to swing by a pet store and pick up two leashes, just in case you would like to exercise your dogs before the long trip to Wisconsin." Now, has Quality Travel differentiated itself from the competition? You bet it has.

By the way, who called the play? Who solved the customer's problem? The employee at Quality Travel got the ball rolling and kept it rolling when it wanted to stop. She didn't settle for making excuses. The rest of the employees at Quality Travel and the manager of the limo service also stepped up and went the extra mile. A good employee can be your greatest weapon.

Did this company excel at the crisis or make excuses as to why they couldn't do something special for the customer?

There is very little difference between people, but the little difference makes a big difference. - W. Clement Stone

What do you think the chances are that this lady will tell her story to others? Let the PWOM begin.

Having a Backup Plan Can Mean Avoiding a Crisis

I am frequently invited to be a keynote speaker at national conferences. The single biggest fear of a meeting planner is that the speaker will not show up due to a flight cancellation or for some other reason. To reduce this risk, my staff never books me on the last flight to the destination; instead, they put me on the second to last flight to ensure that we have a backup. This is added value for the meeting planner. In addition, my team tracks information on the Internet to make sure there is no interruption in my flight plans.

As an example, I was scheduled to do a presentation in Indianapolis, Indiana. My original flight was from Colorado Springs on American Airlines to Dallas, and then from Dallas to Indianapolis. When my staff looked on the Internet for possible situations that could interrupt my flights, they saw that there were active hurricanes off the coast of Florida. They decided to check where the aircraft I would board in Dallas was coming from. When they researched the flight, they saw that the flight was indeed originating in Florida. Even though we had not received notification from the airline, there was a high probability that the aircraft would be delayed or even be unable to leave Florida because of the hurricanes.

The average scenario would have been to leave Colorado Springs and land in Dallas as planned. Then I would have gone to the gate for the outbound flight, and more likely than not I would have heard, "Sorry Mr. Hyden, your flight is canceled. We will get you on a flight tomorrow morning." The meeting planner would then have gotten a call with the news that I was stuck in Dallas and wouldn't be able to get to Indianapolis. Meanwhile, my photo is on the program and the last thing she needs is a call from her keynote speaker saying, "I can't make it."

Anticipating this problem well before I left Colorado Springs, my team immediately rerouted me on a flight from Colorado Springs to O'Hare and then on a connecting flight from O'Hare to Indianapolis. This way I would be certain to get to Indianapolis for the event.

Average would be to blame the airline. If you want to play the game at the awesome level, you have to anticipate what the screw-ups might be and design a Plan B. A Plan B must be designed in advance and be ready to execute when necessity presents itself. My team does this type of anticipation on a regular basis and it is another reason why our clients refer to them as "Team Awesome."

Does your company need to design a Plan B to execute when a potential crisis rears its head?

Few things are harder to put up with than the annoyance of a good example.
- Mark Twain

Average: Wait for a crisis to happen. Employees frown when a crisis hits and then they offer excuses: It's not my fault. It's not my job. I can't do anything about it. I'll have to check with the boss.

Average might be kind. They may need to high jump to get to average. What type of WOM will this generate? NWOM.

Awesome: Your organization needs to anticipate what could go wrong and then design a Plan B so you can "excel at the crisis." Employees smile when a crisis hits; employees never give excuses; employees always go the extra mile; management gets out of the way.

Awesome companies look at a problem as an opportunity to do something special for the customer. What type of WOM will this generate? PWOM.

TOOLS FOR SUPERINTENDENTS.

The employees at Service Directions, the company that sells and maintains laundry machines for apartment owners, came up with a great idea. We were discussing the fact that not all customers who are dissatisfied call the company, write a letter, or tell you in person. These are called "silent dissatisfied customers." When the employees discussed whom the tenant would complain to if they had a problem with the laundry machines, it was obviously not the owner of the facility. They didn't even know who the owner was. So the employees identified the "super" (superintendent) as the most likely person to receive the complaint. The thought was that the super is very visible because he is usually out in the apartment complex fixing sinks, etc., and the tenants typically have a high level of contact with him.

The employees decided that all the supers should have a cell phone to help them relay complaints about service. It would have the phone number of the appropriate individuals at Service Directions and other crucial contact numbers. The supers could then call immediately if there was a problem. They also gave each of the supers a 25-foot tape measure and a five-in-one screwdriver—handy tools that allow for quick, on-the-spot repairs.

The goal was to get to the "silent dissatisfied customers" quickly, because the alternative is that they just might spread NWOM.

Making the change to a customer-focused organization requires leadership at the top. This means more than paying lip service to the philosophy; it requires that management people serve as role models of the desired behaviors.

Too many times, top executives do not respond well in times of crisis. They get tied up in administrative details and delegate the handling of urgent problems to others. This sends the wrong message to employees.

Does your organization "excel at the crisis" or do your leaders and employees give excuses why they can't meet your customer's needs? Average is boring! Does your organization need to develop a Plan B for when a crisis hits?

THANK YOU!

It's a sign of mediocrity when you demonstrate gratitude with moderation. - **Robert Benigni**

ARE MANNERS A LOST ART?

Manners seem to have diminished significantly. My mother and grandmother would roll over in their graves if they saw the lack of manners in today's society. When I was a child, I would be grounded if I didn't say, "Yes, ma'am" or "No, sir." Opening a door for a woman was expected. I think everyone needs to step it up and reconstitute the manners our parents and grandparents taught us.

Customers are the lifeblood of any organization. Without them the organization fails to exist. Following are some opportunities to say "thank you" that you should remember:

Thank You # 1: Thank you for your order.

Even if a customer has been a customer for a long time, if you take them for granted, they may not order again. Saying thank you is the nicest way to say "you are important to me." Also, we all feel good when we receive an email confirming that the company has received our order and another one when they have shipped the order. So keep that in mind.

Thank You # 2: Thank you for your consideration.

If you are in a bidding or quoting situation, it may be prudent to thank the prospect for considering you as a supplier. Who knows, the prospect may

183

consider that an indication of the culture in your company and that may add one more small thing that separates you from the competition. Sometimes it comes down to one more small thing.

Sweat the small stuff.
-Howard

Thank You # 3: Thank you for your input.

You can learn a lot when customers give you feedback. Whether it's a customer satisfaction survey, comments from a focus group, or any other tool that your organization uses to get feedback, thanking the customer for their input is just plain good manners. In addition to a thank you card, you may want to include a note about how you used the information to help raise the bar. It's just good marketing. Not saying "thank you" basically conveys that you are no better off as a result of their feedback.

Thank You # 4: Thank you for your complaint.

Complaints are something that employees frequently duck; they view them as negative. When employees take complaints to management, they think it may get them in trouble. This type of culture can have a huge detrimental effect on the company's competitive advantage. Companies that have an awesome culture of customer focus, encouraging employees to seek out complaints proactively, have a big competitive advantage. There is a huge difference between passively waiting for a complaint, phone call or letter, and having systems in place to proactively find and help dissatisfied customers.

Here's something I crafted for The Care of Trees, a lawn care company: "Complaints are the fertilizer of future growth."

Complaints are an opportunity to learn. - Howard

Thank You # 5: Thank you for your referral.

PWOM can be a substantial marketing opportunity. Would it be prudent to say "thank you" to a customer that gave you a referral? In addition, if the referral turns into a piece of business, it may be appropriate to send a gift along with the thank you. This reinforces the behavior, and perhaps will encourage the customer to refer others. At the very least, it reminds them that you are doing an awesome job and you do appreciate their referrals. I am not a proponent of just soliciting referrals from customers; I'm a strong proponent of the idea that referrals must be earned. If you are not awesome and committed to bringing serious value to your customer, you shouldn't be asking for referrals. After all, would you refer a good friend to someone who's done a mediocre job for you?

Thank You # 6: Thank you for your patience.

I am constantly amazed at the number of companies who are late with a quote for a product or service, or late with a delivery. I think they often believe they got away with it because the phone didn't ring or they didn't receive a letter of complaint. Meanwhile, the customer is fully aware of the fact that they were late. If you want to play the game at the awesome level, it is imperative that you call the customer the minute that you or anyone in your organization knows you are going to be late. Give them a heads-up.

Typically the problem is the internal lack of teamwork from one employee to another. This results in a missed opportunity to give the customer a heads-up. Every person in the organization should know that it is their responsibility to contact the appropriate person in their company and let them know the second they realize something is going to be late. That way, the appropriate person can call the customer and give them a heads-up. Anything short of this is average— not awesome! Calling the customer and saying "thank you for your patience" at least lets the customer know you are on top of it and doing all you can to speed things up.

Thank You # 7: Thank you for a great year.

If your company is thinking about sending Christmas cards, don't. They are typically not worth the paper they are printed on. If you send a Christmas card to the president of a company, the receptionist opens it, staples it to the bulletin board, and the person the card was intended for never reads it. Here is an alternative: send a Thanksgiving Day card. It will stick out because they will only get one or two, and you beat the competition by 30 days.

COME UP WITH CREATIVE WAYS
TO THANK YOUR CUSTOMERS

Service Directions, Inc., in New York, sends all of these types of thank you cards and more. They said, "We send out a Valentine's Day card saying we love our customers." They also send an anniversary card—on the anniversary of first doing business with the customer.

Then they challenged me by saying, "I bet you can't come up with another thank you card." I didn't say a thing; I just made a note: "challenge thank you card." Two weeks later, when I returned to do another workshop, I said to the employees, "I understand that your management team sends out a lot of thank you cards." They all smiled and nodded. I said, "We're not going to take any time during the workshop brainstorming about thank you cards; however, if anyone wants to hang with me after the workshop to brainstorm thank you card ideas, I will buy the soda." About a dozen employees showed up. We brainstormed for about 20 minutes and then an employee jumped up and said, "I've got it. How about a Columbus Day card: 'Thanks for discovering us.'" When I shared this with Steve Jagde, the COO, he proceeded to give me all the accolades. I said, "Stop, I didn't come up with this; one of your employees did. The only difference was I asked them." This story points once again to the fact that management needs to solicit ideas from their employees. If they don't, it's a missed opportunity.

How many thank you cards does your organization have? Another question might be: how many thank you cards does your competitor have? Obviously, you do not need to use all of these thank you cards. However, the absence of thank you cards just might be an indicator of self-centeredness and too much of an internal focus.

How grateful are you for their business? Does your organization need to increase the number of thank you cards you send to customers?

Rate Your Thank You's:

A   B   C   D   E   F

THANK YOU TO OUR EMPLOYEES

As much as we need to thank our customers, we also need to thank our employees. Can you come up with some reasons to say thank you to your employees? Thank you for your input, thank you for your loyalty, thank you for joining our organization, or just plain thanks for being on our team.

THANK YOU TO OUR CUSTOMERS

And finally, thank you to our customers and the other awesome companies whose stories have helped us bring more value to the content of this book:

What is your organization's manners quotient? Do you take your customers for granted or does your organization have numerous ways to say "thank you" to customers and employees? And if you do have numerous ways to say "thank you," do you use them effectively? What kind of rating would your grandmother or mother give you? Hmmm . . .

3M
2J Supply
AGEC – Applied Geotechnical Engineering Consultants
Anheuser-Busch
APG Cash Drawer
Apple
Boeing Company
Blinds.com
Builders Appliance Center
Care of Trees
CFSAA – Casket & Funeral Supply Assn. Of America
Data Aire
Del Webb
Direct Tire & Auto Service
Domino's Pizza
Dunn Lumber
eBags
FedEx
Gaftek
Ivy Acres

Nordstrom
NorthStar Print Group
Northwest Airlines
PCCA – Professional Compounding Centers of America
PCCA Australia
PEI – Petroleum Equipment Institute
Perry's Ice Cream
Procter & Gamble
Progress Supply
Quality Travel
Raymond Handling Solutions
Ritz Carlton
Sandhill Scientific
Service Directions
Southwest Airlines
Tomar Electronics
Tuffy Muffler
TEC – The Executive Committee
Vistage International
Volvo
WalMart
Westrec Marinas
Whitsons Culinary Group
Wrigley Gum

In the end it all comes down to one thing:

ADD VALUE OR STAY HOME!

HOWARD

AFTERWORD

Our company was introduced to Howard Hyden back in 2001. In March of that year, we invited Howard to introduce his customer focus ideas to our entire organization. At that time we had about 170 employees, so we had to break into several sessions to get everyone involved and engaged.

Howard gave us the idea of approaching all challenges and opportunities, as well as policies and procedure, with the benefit to the customer in mind. He calls this "outside-in" thinking. Most companies set things up to benefit themselves and hope that the customers somehow get what they want. That's "inside-out." Howard got us busy working on ideas to help PCCA rethink everything we do to make it "outside-in." Howard can certainly keep a crowd alive. His chant is, "Dare to be awesome!"

One of PCCA's competitive advantages is its intense culture of service expressed in the team vision: "Go the extra mile, all of the time. Do whatever it takes, whenever it's needed. Astonish customers every day. And always remember, we're in this together!" The level of customer loyalty PCCA enjoys can only be explained by the customer attraction or customer affinity such a culture elicits.

The concepts of putting the customer in the center of all decisions and actions in the company should not have been a revelation to a team so dedicated to service. However, the experience was nothing short of revolutionary as the team began to use the tools they were already familiar with in new applications and on projects never before imagined. There is no doubt that having an "outside-in" approach can shift every molecule in the decision-brain to create an outcome that will boost customer satisfaction.

We did a lot in a very short period of time and literally had everyone engaged in generating ideas about how to be more "outside-in." We compiled the lists of ideas and then disseminated them in areas we wanted to act upon:

- Things that we could do immediately; those were our "just do it" list.

- Items we wanted to do right away, but had to do more planning before we could execute them.

- Items that we wanted to explore in greater detail and determine if we should do them.

- Items that we may want to do, but not now; a "someday maybe" list.

We reconnected with Howard in the summer of 2006 to see if there was a "next level" of opportunity for us to improve. Howard's recommendation was that we take a group of our key executives and teach them a process for driving customer focus principles deeper into our organization. Howard called this the "Corporate Culture Workshop."

In essence, it taught us how to take the customer focus program and make sure we keep upping the game in our culture. Executives took the fundamental activities of our company and examined how we might better infuse "outside-in" thinking into all of them on a continuous basis. We looked at areas like strategic planning, internal and external communications, human resources, employee satisfaction, training, operations, how we learn from our customers, and our review and measurement systems.

All this is to build accountability into our organization and to imprint customer focus on our company DNA. Oh, how I wish we could have picked up on this process a few years earlier when we were tasked to bring a sales approach into our culture. We already had a super service culture and we wanted to tie a sales mentality to it. Those of you who have tried to make something happen in your organization that represents a cultural shift recognize that this is one of the most difficult feats to pull off. What happened is a methodology that we can use for anything that we need to make happen throughout the company and have it stick.

So did all of this energy pay off? Well, we attribute the timeliness of Howard's work with us to having had a significant impact. From 2001 through 2009, PCCA has tripled its revenues and doubled its return on sales with profit dollars up fourfold! We have gone from an estimated 35% to an estimated 50% of the market share and have hundreds and hundreds of raving fan clients. Certainly a myriad of other key factors contributed to PCCA's success during this time frame, but ultimately it has been PCCA's continued efforts to keep looking at how it does business with an "outside-in" frame of mind that has paid off in customer loyalty.

We thank Howard for investing the energy and talent to help PCCA's staff ensure that we are a world class service organization. While widget companies could certainly benefit from Howard's Customer Focus principles as well, PCCA has used them to bring relief to countless patients (both human and animal) by serving its community pharmacist members. Thanks to PCCA and Howard Hyden, compounding pharmacy is back to its roots of individualized care as a profession and is definitely Customer Focused!

It's fun to get a call from Howard and have him say, "Is anyone over there awesome?" and be able to say, "PCCA is awesome." Hang out with Howard Hyden, and you'll make a big leap toward being truly awesome for all your company's employees, customers and stakeholders.

Jim Smith, President
PCCA, Professional Compounding
Centers of America